HOW TO NOT
RUIN
YOUR KIDS WITH MONEY

HOW TO NOT RUIN YOUR KIDS WITH MONEY

MARK A. SHILLER

Published and distributed by:
Aevitas Press
Milwaukee, Wisconsin, USA
inquiries@aevitaspress.com
www.aevitaspress.com

First Edition, April 2024
Copyright, Mark A. Shiller

How to Not Ruin Your Kids with Money
Aevitas Press
979-8-9900329-0-3 hardcover
979-8-9900329-1-0 paperback
979-8-9900329-2-7 ebook

To every parent who's doing their best
to raise decent human beings.

Table of Contents

About the Author

Mark Shiller has been helping families manage the personal, financial, and legal aspects of intergenerational transfers of wealth throughout his 30-year career as an estate and business succession planning attorney. In that time, he has collaborated with some of the most creative and engaging minds in the field - and he includes many of his wonderful clients in that list. Maintaining a posture of openness and intellectual curiosity in both his personal and professional life has allowed for deeper and more successful engagements with families pursuing positive outcomes with wealth transfers – even when the odds might seem stacked against them.

His professional success in these matters and his knack for explaining complex topics and connecting them to real world solutions has made Mark a sought-after speaker and led to time as a member of the National Trust School faculty of the American Bankers Association and as an adjunct professor at the University of Wisconsin Law School. He's become known as someone who gets to the heart of the matter and addresses the tough stuff with compassion, empathy and optimism. Audiences and those who bring Mark in to speak also appreciate the humor he brings to every speech, workshop and interaction with him — no doubt enhanced in part due to his continuing, over 20-year "side hustle" as a professional improv comedian with the national comedy troupe, Fish Sticks Comedy.

Mark lives just outside of Milwaukee, Wisconsin with his wife, Jennifer, in their home that also used to house their four now adult children, Max, Bennett, Zach and Annie.

Acknowledgements

Completing a book is a shared accomplishment – especially when the subject is as core to the author's professional values and activities as is the case here. Professionally, I have far too many to list who have given of themselves in ways that have shaped me as lawyer and as an advisor. I have had them "top of mind" throughout the writing process.

With respect to the book itself, I want to thank Jennifer Milton-Houlton for her thoughtful editing and encouragement. Thanks, too, to my wonderful beta readers, John Lyche, Joe Schlidt, Dean Fowler, and Tom Deans. Each contributed different insights and challenges and suggested adjustments that were quite significant and meaningful to the final manuscript. My wife, Jen, and my son, Bennett, also were kind enough to do their own reading of the initial draft and shared meaningful and illuminating comments.

My wife has been an incredible supporter of this project, even though it required sacrifices of my time and personal focus to reach its conclusion. This book doesn't happen without her.

Lastly, I want to thank my own "Next Gens" – Max, Bennett, Zach and Annie. I'm so proud of each of them and how they're thriving in the Danger Zone (you'll see what I mean soon enough). Thank you for allowing me to share part of our story and your stories in these pages.

Mark Shiller

Disclaimers and Guidance

We're about to have a very personal conversation. I'll share many stories, examples, patterns, successes, and failures in the pages that follow. As I do, I'm mindful of the importance of maintaining confidentiality of particular circumstances and things specific to one individual or family situation. There were many points in my writing where I realized that laying out certain patterns and commonalities could lead some readers to think that a certain story I share here is "theirs." And to a certain extent, they are. Except with respect to what I share from my own life, though, almost everything shared will be amalgamations of quite a number of situations that I have personally been involved in or "in the know" about. So if you see yourself at any point in these pages - whether we know each other or not - know that I'm almost certainly talking about many, many people who had a similar experience to your own.

As you work through the text, you will likely discern that a lot of the strategies and approaches to dealing with the impact of wealth transfers have been worked out within the context of High Net Worth ("HNW") or Ultra High Net Worth ("UHNW") individuals and families. Not all. But a lot. Even so, while some aspects of what we discuss might apply only to HNW or UHNW individuals and families, and some issues will land harder on those with larger wealth, the large majority of what we will cover will apply to everyone who might be considered generally at least a bit affluent.

It may help you to have a sense of where you sit within these various subgroups before diving in. Where the categories start and stop vary depending on who you ask,[1] but for our purposes, I think of things in three categories, with 2024 (the year of publishing) net worth amounts in the United States included to help contextualize these – (1) Affluent, sometimes referred to as the "Mass Affluent" in the financial services industry – are those with a net worth of roughly $1 Million to about $10 Million; (2) HNW – representing those with a net worth of $10 Million to somewhere between $30 Million and $50 Million; and (3) UHNW – representing those with net worth in excess of those in categories 1 and 2. There are further breakpoints in the UHNW category – most of which do not have too much impact on the conversation that follows. Now that you know where you slot in, let me give you some guidance in advance about how to approach this book based on your category:

---

1 The Charles Schwab Modern Wealth Survey 2023 states that Americans say that a net worth of $2.2 Million will result in someone being considered wealthy. See, https://content.schwab.com/web/retail/public/about-schwab/schwab_modern_wealth_survey_2023_findings.pdf to see the fuller results. It's an interesting read.

Affluent

If you are in the first category, you probably have to resist the temptation to do what many in your situation do – dismiss many or all of the issues we'll discuss as only relevant for those with more money than you have. Affluent and HNW people often seem predisposed to view themselves as not be worth enough for full planning. Sure, you may be able to accomplish wealth transfers without the same level of tax planning that those in the HNW or UHNW context might require, but you still need to consider the implications of future wealth transfers on your children or other beneficiaries. You might need to "drive the bus" a bit more than those with more wealth, but this book should give you a good road map about how to get where you'll want to go. Keep a notebook nearby and write down things that you might need to take on or explore further.

High Net Worth

HNW individuals and families will definitely benefit from the road map laid out in this book. If this is where you and/or your family land, you are likely to have some additional resources available to you from the advisors you are more likely to have or have access to. There may be a temptation to over-rely on these advisors, but also a tension as to how much to invest in outside specialists beyond the standard retention of attorneys, accountants, investment advisors, etc. Regardless, you too will need to be driving some of the important work required for successful wealth transfers. So keep the keys to the bus in your hand as you read this book as well.

Ultra High Net Worth

Most UHNW folks will not be dismissive of the need for this planning – but are most at risk for over-delegating tasks to their advisors. Life tends to get more complicated financially with greater wealth, so there is an aspect of delegation that naturally occurs. It sometimes is a necessity to keep things rolling. The predisposition to pass along tasks to others then becomes more natural. You'll see, though, that the subject we're working through in these pages is inherently and highly personal. So even if you can afford a driver, you should keep a hold on the keys and you should set the course for you and your family.

I've written this book for anyone who has enough wealth to potentially do damage to their heirs if gifts or inheritances aren't managed well. Even someone with a net worth under all three of the above categories could therefore find important value in working through the issues we'll work through together in this book. Just like you can drown in an inch of water in a bathtub, a few thousand dollars at the wrong time to someone not then ready for it can lead to catastrophic outcomes. I therefore hope all readers will benefit from this conversation's objective of closing the access and information gap on working smartly on wealth transitions.

Preface

Y ou're holding in your hands a book entitled *How to Not Ruin Your Kids with Money*. That must mean you've got at least a bit of wealth and at least a bit of worry about how that wealth will affect those you most love and care about. And the greater the wealth you have, I suspect the greater the worry is, too. Maybe your kids are far enough along and doing well enough that your concerns about them have diminished – but these same worries and concerns then become focused on grand-children and generations further down the line.

You probably haven't had a lot of conversations about these matters. Few do. Fewer still have a good handle on what they can do to resolve the underlying issues. So it's no surprise that families continue to struggle with transfers of wealth. It's simply hard not to ruin your kids with money.

I've been walking side-by-side with families as they tackle these concerns for three decades now. In that time, I've seen many approaches to resolving the "trust fund baby" problem: elegant trust structures and tax strategies, thoughtful analysis of managing intra-family governance, robust investment allocations, unique business development strategies for next gens, and so on. Many bring some level of benefit to parents' efforts to successfully transition their wealth to their children and later generations. You should explore and consider all of them. But something more is needed if you are going to "parent well with wealth."

Success in this area requires you to approach things differently. More wholistically. And maybe with a lot more personal engagement. While there isn't a magic formula, there is a better way. Having seen families experience successful wealth transitions and put themselves in position for future successes, I am excited to share with you strategies, principles and activities that will set you and your family up to achieve better, more satisfying results than families of wealth typically experience.

I'm anxious to get started – but a few caveats before we begin. Keep in mind that I'm not a psychologist. I'm not a financial planner, investment professional or CPA. And even though I have been an estate and business succession planning attorney my whole career, I don't intend to get into the technical in's and out's of establishing effective tax strategies or trust structures and the like in this book. I'm hoping you have or find solid professionals who can be of great value to you on these and other relevant topics. You need them. But what you also need is an understanding of the base, human level issues that make wealth transitions hard, a framework to establish what goals and strategies will serve you well, and then a pathway to transferring wealth well across generations. We're going to get into all of that here.

In addition, I very much recognize that everyone's situation is unique. You and your spouse might have been happily married for 50 years and have 2.3 perfect children who are on the same path you've taken. But just as likely, your family might be made up of members that aren't the product of a single marriage or even any marriage at all. Or one of a million different structures and combinations that form your family. The principles and challenges remain the same – but specific points, examples or goals might not be perfect fits. There were many, many points in this book where I felt like those misalignments for some family structures needed a call out to point out that there are limits to this statement or that. That could be a by-product of my legal training and the professional environment I've been in most of my adult life. Regardless, for readability, I've tried to control this impulse to account for every nuance and will ask for your forgiveness for anywhere where your personal circumstances aren't fully covered.

OK. I've got my cup of coffee and am ready to spend some time with you. Get what you need, but settle in and let's see what we can do to set you and your family up for success!

Define the Problem

PART ONE

Living with Wealth

The popular narrative regarding wealth is that life is easier, fuller, and more worry-free with more of it than with less. The individual's experience is usually quite different. Not that life can't be full and pleasant with significant wealth. Of course it can. But wealth comes with its share of responsibilities and burdens, too.

One of the most consistent by-products of having wealth is the negative impact wealth has on nearly all relationships. It doesn't help that the implications and effects don't get talked about outside of the home. Heck, it's often not even addressed within the home. Breaking through and actually engaging on this topic often seems to require creating an environment where it's OK to "complain" about the negatives that accompany wealth. Perhaps there's a concern of being perceived as ungrateful or self-centered. Whatever it is, people often have a hard time getting comfortable with even having the discussion.

Over the years I've worked with and known a lot of wealth creators who for one reason or another have been able to grow their balance sheets larger than those of most or all of their neighbors, friends and family. I've also worked with and know many children and grandchildren who have been around and received wealth through gifts and inheritances. No question that there are positives that go along with that experience. But we should also recognize the pretty big downsides that come with increased wealth. Things like isolation. Expectations. Jealousies.

I live in Milwaukee. In 2015, our town had front row seats to one of the clearest, public examples of how the downsides to wealth can impact someone. At that time, the NBA's Milwaukee Bucks had a basketball player on their roster named Larry Sanders. He was a first-round draft pick in 2010 and was playing a significant role at the game's highest level very quickly. He had such a strong start that in 2013 the Bucks signed him to a $44 million contract extension. He was a rising star. And rising fast. But in 2015, at the age of 26, with $27 million due him if he just continued to play, Larry Sanders simply, and suddenly, walked away. From the outside looking in, it was a stunning decision.

Not long after he left professional basketball, Larry put out an online article along with a video interview to address the rampant speculation about his decision to leave the game. According to Larry, "I've never chased money. It's never been how I define success. Happiness isn't behind a golden gate." At the same time, he acknowledged that having money impacted his life significantly.

As with many (but not all) athletes, Larry Sanders' contract put him in a financially different category from those that he grew up with. He put it like this:

> *You come into the league, you get dropped this large amount of money out of nowhere. People automatically change around you. That just happens. You become an ATM to some people. You have to be correct in your statements. You have to state things a certain way. You give up your freedom of speech, for real. You really can't say how you feel. There's no one really, you know, trying to guide, teach you what you should do and shouldn't do.[2]*

Although most of my clients don't make $44 million with a single signature in their mid-20's, Larry Sanders' experience sounds a lot like the experience of those with significant wealth on so many levels. Wealth coming quickly is jarring – particularly when it is "dropped on" a young person who has not fully established themself and their philosophies and approach to wealth. Whether it comes fast or slow, though, having wealth definitely impacts the relationships with the one who has it – and even of those who are near it.

How does this work out in real life? How do people "change around you," to use Larry's words? Here are a few things that I've seen:

Money Magnifies and Reveals Character

It has been apparent to me for decades that money magnifies character. This proves true not only as to the holder of the money (i.e., wealth), but also for those who are in that

---

2   *Why I Walked Away* From the NBA, Larry Sanders, February 26, 2015, https://www.theplayerstribune.com/articles/larry-sanders-exclusive-interview.

person's world. And the more money involved, the greater the magnification of character. A little money may not be enough to lead to a noticeable issue with greed, covetousness, or pride. But a large amount of money is almost surely to reveal these or similar character deficiencies. Sometimes in spectacular and horrifying fashion.

There are too many examples that we could consider regarding lottery winners whose marriages and families fell apart, that used their money on drugs or sex or whatever, and a host of other tragedies. I thought about referencing specific stories that have hit the news for other reasons, too – but decided against it. Yes, these stories might be a warning signal and illustrate a point. But they're also stories about human beings who had flaws within themselves or their families that were set ablaze by the financial kerosene of overwhelming wealth all at once. Here's the thing: we all (yes, even your sweet, lovely, 5-year-old granddaughter) are human beings who have flaws that could be amplified negatively by wealth.

Big Disparities in Wealth Lead To Envy

Let's continue in this discussion by talking about someone who many consider to have handled sudden wealth well: Sandra Hayes. Sandra was a single mother who worked for the government of the State of Missouri government that won approximately $10 million in a lottery in 2006. She made a few "dream purchases," but also got some financial advice to prudently invest the rest and reportedly has lived well within her financial means ever since.

That didn't mean all was easy for her. According to Sandra,

I had to endure the greed and the need that people have, trying to get you to release your money to them. That caused a lot of emotional pain. These are people who you've loved deep down, and they're turning into vampires trying to suck the life out of me.[3]

That's strong language. Yet those with significant wealth (remember: what is considered significant can vary significantly from one person to the next) can instantly bring to mind several "vampires" in their lives. These vampires are not just envious. They look for opportunities to suck some of the wealth out of their wealthy family member or friend. Some are shockingly bold about it and might even start to feel entitled to it. Which is confusing and hurtful.

Of course, this experience is not limited to lottery winners whose wealth is broadcast to the world on the evening news. It is common among business owners, property owners, heirs & heiresses, employees of public and private companies whose options hit big, professional athletes, top actors, and so on. It's one reason so many millionaires decide to be the Millionaire Next Door, as described by authors, Thomas Stanley and William Danko in the book of the same name. A modest lifestyle is surprisingly effective camouflage for vampires.

Wealth Makes it Hard to Know Whose Motives are Pure

Not everyone is a vampire, of course. But not every vampire wears a cape and shows their fangs when they smile.

---

3   "Big winners share lessons, risks of Powerball win," by Andrew Scherzaiger, November 28, 2012 edition of USA Today.

It seems to me that the uncertainty about who in your life might eventually show themselves to be a vampire and who won't is one of the most disconcerting aspects of relationships for people with wealth. At least as it relates to relationships with those of less wealth.

Suspicion about who a person is or isn't can easily find its way into just about any relationship. It might start with an innocent decision to pick up the check for dinner or drinks – or someone's delay to reach for it -- which then leads to an expectation that the wealthier person will pick it up the next time, and the next, and then forever. Maybe the person lets the wealthier person pick up the check each time because they figure they want to. Or maybe they expect (or begin to expect) that they will pick up the check because their wealthy friend "should."

I wish I could say this suspicion dissipates over time. Instead it usually grows and eventually leads to barriers in relationships. "Wealthy people" seem to (1) resign themselves to the fact that they usually won't know for sure whether anyone's motives to be in relationship are just for themselves as a person; (2) withdraw (emotionally or fully) from relationships with people of significantly different wealth levels; or (3) milk it for the attention and appearance of closeness. Each of the three have their drawbacks, but they also can layer into each other. For instance, we all deep down crave personal, positive connection. But if you feel you can't know if you have a real friendship with someone and/or you've kept yourself emotionally pulled back, you might try to mask the loneliness by using your wealth to draw others to play the part of the friend or confidant. These saccharin relationships, after all, can feel real at least for a little while.

I don't know why I have had so many "first time" conversations on this particular experience. As honored as I've been to be allowed into these discussions, it is concerning how alone people are regarding this topic. No doubt many hold back out of fear that they will be perceived as judgmental or too suspicious of others. Hopefully, though, these conversations can be normalized and held more frequently.

In a healthy situation, disparities of wealth should have no impact on the quality of the relationship. Each person should be evaluated for who they are and friendship and care for one another should be unaffected by how much or how little anyone might own in the moment, next year, or way down the road.[4] But the realities of interpersonal relationships are what they are.

Discomfort and Shame Leads to Reduced Transparency

Some people are very comfortable with showing their wealth in what they wear, what they drive, the homes they live in, and so on. Others are not. Watch enough movies or television shows, and you'll see that the wealthy are often portrayed in a negative light – conniving, manipulative,

---

4   Let me acknowledge that there is a flip side to this issue which is probably worth mentioning here, even though the focus of the book is more about how those with wealth deal with the consequences of having it. Those with less wealth can also have difficulties with relationships with wealthier people. One way this can play out is when the unwealthy person is "over-helped." There can be a type of pity that can be quite demoralizing, even dehumanizing, for someone who has relatively very little to be treated as dependent on others. They want to be recognized as full human beings, too, without regard to what they have and without regard to what they don't have.

greedy, selfish. Sometimes they're portrayed as dumb, aloof, and unaware. Sure, they most often come around at the end of the movie in the common "I got more from you than I ever could have given to you" scene – but for the most part movies generally portray the wealthy characters quite poorly. That cultural aspect may lead a wealthy person to feel uncomfortable about revealing their wealth.

When the money comes suddenly, the vampires may use one of their greatest weapons – "You weren't this way before ..." – to project shame onto their prey. These attacks can be jarring at first and may cause a sense of shame to grow and metastasize. This can then prove effective at loosening the purse strings. Maybe we need to be better at evaluating our own character. Perhaps they're right on some level. But whether we need to be more self-critical, internalizing the shame that comes with even wondering whether the vampires are right is consequential. And once shame is internalized, it is difficult to rid oneself of it.

We talked about isolation above. This type of shame is another factor that leads to isolation. A wealthy person might not want to talk about it because who is going to feel sorry for the rich guy/gal/kid? If the answer you give yourself is no one, then you've just provided fuel for that shame to grow and spread. This will eventually leak out in various, mostly unhealthy, ways.

Your experience with any individual friend, family member, or neighbor, may be very different. I hope you have plenty of people in your life where you do not have any of the concerns discussed above. In my experience, though, the greater the level of wealth and/or the greater the disparity of wealth with others makes it much more likely that some or all the above concerns will manifest themselves. Has that been true for you?

After thinking about your relationships, stop for a second and consider the above in light of various stages of life for your children. I don't have any overwhelming insight for you on what impact wealth has on the youngest children, whether for good or for bad – but it does seem clear that the impact is significantly muted by lack of awareness. Think of the pre-teen or teen whose family suddenly comes into money. They have to deal with all the above concerns with a (typically much) reduced ability to process what's going on internally and with those around them. So, if the above resonates with you and your experience, how do you think it played out or is playing out for your kids?

I suspect that many, probably most, readers will pick up this book when some or all of their children are at least young adults. Perhaps you discussed these topics with your children in advance of that life stage. Most don't, though. That doesn't mean your 12-year-old didn't avoid being viewed differently when their classmates realized that you drove different cars, or lived in a different kind of home, or took different vacations. Your kid may have become "different" and "other" without even realizing it or at least understanding why. It can be a confusing experience for them.

How being viewed as different from others impacts the maturation process is usually very individualized. Maybe more so because most children of wealth typically walk this road alone. Not only do they have to navigate the impact of being within a family of wealth on their own character, though, but do so with the distortions that wealth visits on their relationships with others.

We'll talk more about the impact of wealth on "the kids" as we move further on in our conversation. Before closing out this chapter, though, I want to reiterate an important point alluded to above: It's not just the ownership of the assets that creates the issues described above. Knowledge of the wealth that is, or will eventually become, available can be just as or perhaps more damaging to the financial maturation process. Don't be lulled to sleep by the fact that you're going to live for a long time before your children inherit from you when they're in their 80's. The presence of wealth in a family system can prove just as damaging or more to the kids or grandkids even when direct access, control or ownership is deferred for many, many years.

NOTE TO NEXT GENS

Along the way I'll carve out a few spots to speak directly to those readers who are "Next Gens." By Next Gens I mean those who are in line to inherit/assume the primary wealth stewardship position in the family in the future. If that's you, there are two perspectives that you should keep in mind when reading this book – 1) as the recipient of the wealth from prior generation(s); and (2) as a parent/future parent of later inheritors. In this book, I'm definitely speaking more towards the latter perspective. There's plenty in here for you as a recipient, but it might help to keep a few things in mind as you continue on:

1. As we explore aspects of human nature that can lead to negative outcomes, do not lose track of this book's underlying belief that positive outcomes are not only possible but very much achievable.

2. Relatedly, when we talk about things like "shirtsleeves to shirtsleeves in three generations," like we will in the next chapter, I am hoping to create increased understanding and awareness of challenges. I am not making predictions or prophecies about you or anyone in your family.

3. Your agency, contributions and example will be central and necessary to the successful generational transfers of wealth within your family.

Bottom line – if you are reading this book to determine whether it provides a fair or unfair critique of you and your attitudes on wealth, I suggest you'll miss a lot. I encourage you instead to engage in this conversation looking for pathways to success. I'm confident you'll see plenty of that in the pages ahead if you're open to it.

2

Human Nature
of the Problem

Did reading the previous chapter get you more worried? Do you wonder whether the inheritance you will leave to your kids will make their lives harder? Or whether passing on wealth to your kids be positive or negative? And what about the grandkids? How will having additional wealth impact them?

Even though these are natural and common concerns, almost the only strategy offered by estate planners to positively transition wealth to the next generation to date is to delay when the next generation receives it. Hold the assets in trust longer. Give the kids control over their inheritance later in life - or maybe not at all. We've had a lot of bright minds thinking about these issues for a long time and we've certainly heard plenty of cautionary tales and seen enough bad results that we could learn from. Kicking the can down the road seems like just about all we've come up with. And so the problem persists.

Perhaps you have heard the proverb attributed to Andrew Carnegie: Shirtsleeves to shirtsleeves in three generations. What you may not know is that this sentiment is reflected in many cultures, both Eastern and Western – some dating back as long as 3,000 years (rice paddy to rice paddy in three generations is a Chinese version that may date back that far). This "collection" of such similar proverbial sayings is sometimes referred to as the "Three Generations Rule." For me, the commonality of this concept across time, culture and geography suggests that we are dealing with a universal, human tendency that wealth does not naturally sustain itself across generations. Rather, it would appear that humans have significant challenges to passing wealth to, or past, the grandchildren's generation.[5]

We need to acknowledge that we're swimming upstream if we want to pass wealth generationally. Swimming upstream is hard. And the more wealth there is, the stronger the current pushes against us. I may not need to tell you that -- but I might need to remind you, as many people of wealth seem to forget. Before we go a little further it will probably help to consider several strikes that we have against us:

---

5   There is much more work to be done to determine how and how strong this pattern might be in current contexts and cultures. For instance, the dramatic build up in wealth that has occurred in the past 100 years, going all the way from shirtsleeves to shirtsleeves is less likely in just three generations. Larger piles of wealth might just take longer to dissipate. Regardless, while I find the diminishment of wealth across generations a very interesting subject, I will not be digging deeply into it in this book. If you would like to explore these matters in greater depth, I suggest checking out *Family Wealth* and other works by James E. "Jay" Hughes Jr. and other works on wealth transitions across generations. I intend to maintain a list of resources at www.markshiller.com/resources/ if you would like to explore this and other like subjects addressed in this book. You're also welcome to suggest others that impacted you by emailing me at mark@markshiller.com.

Successful Wealth Transfer Is Difficult

Because we're swimming upstream and against human nature, we also have to acknowledge that we have our own human nature fighting against us. And what do we tend to do with things that are hard? We put them off. We ignore them. We live in denial. We look for easy fixes. We look for people to tell us it'll all be OK. None of those approaches work very well. But we do them anyway – many times unknowingly or unconsciously.

There Aren't Many Role Models

How many examples can you come up with within your family or close social circles of wealth transitioned well? I hope you have some good ones to point to, but most people have just a few and many none. That could be because we tend to remember and notice the negative more than the positive, but I've not met anyone that has only experienced and been around successful generational wealth transfers.

If you're a wealth creator, the odds are fairly high that you will (or at least could) leave more wealth to your children than your parents will leave (or may have left) for you. Some of that has to do with the incredible buildup of wealth in many societies over the past 100 years. Although the distribution of that wealth has not been shared evenly across any society, in 2024 you are more likely to be in a better financial position than your parents were/are and that your parents were/are in a better financial position than their parents/your grandparents. Accordingly, one reason you are less likely to have a close role model on this subject is that your ancestors didn't walk the same road you're walking now.

Advisors Can't Do It All, But We So Want Them To

We'll talk about how to get the most out of your professional advisors in Chapter 13, but here's the reality: you can't outsource everything regarding transferring wealth well and expect success. The achievement of successful generational transfers of wealth requires effort from you and members of your family. Any success or failure will be yours and your family's. Not any advisor's.

As obvious as I suspect that it sounds, it is so very like us humans to want to have the problem magically solved. It can be so tempting to sign up for this advisor or that advisor's program or service to resolve whatever challenges we might face. I've seen it play out hundreds of times – probably more within the legal profession, but not just. Let me give you an example of what I mean:

A couple comes into the lawyer's office. They've known the lawyer since early on in their business life, and she's provided helpful advice as their business has experienced incredible success. The business is still growing, and it's expected to grow by leaps and bounds over the next 10 to 20 years. As the kids are getting older and starting their own families, the couple knows they need to address their estate plan.

In discussing the options, it is recommended that the couple transfer a portion of the company to an irrevocable trust for the benefit of the children. The couple agrees but are concerned about what that might mean to their children and grandchildren given that these trusts could quickly be worth tens, maybe hundreds, of millions of dollars. To address these concerns, the lawyer suggests the following:

1. Have a third party serve as trustee so that the kids aren't in control right away (perhaps ever).

2. Keep it quiet as to how much is in the trust during the couple's lifetime.

3. Don't plan on making distributions at all, or at least not distributions of any consequence, during the couple's lifetime.

And that's what they do. Following the lawyer's recommendations feels safe, and they can see how it could save millions of dollars in estate and gift taxes. The couple has done something directly addressing the issue at hand and leaves the office feeling as though a weight has been lifted.

Fast forward 20 or 30 years. The company performed quite well, and accordingly, so did the trust. The children are now in their 50's or 60's, but likely have little sense of what the trust means to them. And probably feel like it never really will matter all that much to them even after their parents pass away. After all, since the trust was their parents' project and not really "theirs," the children had to figure out how to make their own way in life independent of the trust. Sure, they likely had plenty of advantages from mom and dad, but not anywhere near the scope of what the wealth held within the trust could have provided. At the same time, as detached as the children might feel from this plan, the parents likely view the trust's growth as indicative of successful planning and provision for the family.

In situations like these, the senior generation – in this case represented by the parents – has emotionally benefited from the feeling that things are taken care of. The next generation – in this case the children – are often bystanders and beneficiaries more in name than in actuality. So, their lives don't change and the trust is more Mom and Dad's "thing" than theirs. It likely will end up being a more meaningful resource after the senior generation's death – and more likely a resource of greater consequence to the third generation than the children's generation. And, as alluded to above, that's where things tend to fall apart.

Is the great plan still a great plan in 20 years or more? From a tax avoidance perspective it sure is. But from a family perspective, from a personal perspective, from a human perspective, we don't really know. There's a significant chance that the "people" and "relational" results will be disappointing. And maybe terribly so.

Does this mean that advisors in examples like these gave bad advice at the outset? Probably not. At least not fully or even mostly. A tax concern was addressed, and it likely felt good to all involved in the initial transaction to tackle a real and present issue. And years later the plan's success in avoiding taxes or other concerns could clearly be viewed as having worked better than advertised on the front end. While the advice may have therefore been quite good on these points, how other considerations play out over time are likely to have a greater impact on whether any strategy can truly be viewed as a success.

It's Easy to "Pass the Buck"

As much as we feel responsibility for how our kids turn out, how they do is not solely on us. Yes, parents can and do have a significant impact on their children's character and life choices. And there's no question we can really do a number on our children, too. But ultimately, if we discount the worst parenting from the equation, each individual ultimately has responsibility and accountability for themselves and decides for themselves how much good or bad influence to accept from their parents and others. So, if someone doesn't live up to our hopes or expectations, is it on them? Or on us?

Of course, it's not as simple as that. Little in life is that binary. Parents and grandparents do influence the next generations and are responsible for how they wield that influence. But children and grandchildren are also responsible for their life choices and character. There is a mutuality of responsibility among the generations in a family – and therefore a communal shared success or failure between all members of a family. I recognize that various cultures might strike different balances between how individual or communal relationships are viewed. Yet, how we walk through life always has an impact on those around us – particularly our closest family members.

It Just Isn't Fun

I've seen statistics suggesting that people spend, on average, an hour or two on their estate planning. That's not an hour or two each year. That's across a person's entire lifetime. Shockingly, that means what a person accumulates over their lifetime usually gets almost no meaningful attention. At all. To take it a step further, even those who have pursued sophisticated estate and financial planning generally haven't spent that much more time on the subject. Heck, even if you spent 50 times the average, that's still a really small amount of focus on a topic that will significantly impact those you care most about in your immediate descendants and the generations that will follow.

As much as I enjoy working with people on their planning, I'd be lying if I said I haven't heard people tell me that they just don't enjoy much of the process. Thinking about one's death or the death of a loved one is disconcerting and uncomfortable to some. I'm also aware that only a modest percentage of the world is drawn to working through the legalese and the four-dimensional structures[6] created by advisors. A larger percentage – but not anywhere close to half – want to dive into their investment statements and individual holdings. And let's not get into the untold joy in reading tax returns and financial statements right now. Those who see any of these as dry and confusing also know that it makes it really easy to focus on something else.

> One reason that people don't tend to their estate planning more is that they assume it's more important for people that have much more wealth than they do. Even though that's not sound thinking as issues surrounding wealth transitions impact just about everyone, it is a persistent sentiment. Don't get caught in the trap thinking that it's not something you need to think about.

And there will be other reasons to avoid things tomorrow. And the day after that. And so on.

---

6   Time is usually an under-considered dimension in an estate plan.

It's Just So Darn Confusing

The fact that you're reading this book probably means that you've either done some estate planning or have at least thought hard about tackling the subject. If you've put together a Will and Revocable Trust, you probably have a really nice binder that contains copies of all the intricate documents that your legal counsel created for you. Maybe you've organized your investments and kept up with the reports and recommendations and perspective of your investment advisors, too. But, if you're like many, you still worry that something isn't covered. It feels like something has been left undone.

One reason that might be so is that even if you've gotten the best of the best advice from all your advisors, your planning can feel incomplete if you don't feel certain that it addresses what's most important to you. We'll discuss this in greater depth later in the book, but if you don't know how your plan furthers your desires for your spouse, your children, your grandchildren, your community, etc., then you'll be left with uncertainty and confusion as to whether it will positively work towards your goals.

Beyond that, the complexities of life and wealth management are ever increasing and can make us all feel pretty stupid. I know this, because many smart and accomplished people tell me all the time that they feel dumb when it comes to estate planning, or financial planning, or taxes, or whatever. There's no shame in walking into a lawyer's office without understanding the nuances of the Chapter 14 Special Valuation Rules under the Internal Revenue Code – yet for some reason, people hold themselves to an impossibly high standard of understanding intricate and sophisticated tax and financial matters and are embarrassed that they don't. Best to let go of that if you can. Give yourself a break.

The other side, though, of "feeling dumb" on a topic is that it can also make you feel vulnerable. As an analogy, I know a bit about cars, but not a heck of a lot. If I take my car in for service and am told I need a part that I've never heard of before to get the car back on the road, I am almost completely vulnerable to what the mechanic says needs to be done and what he or she tells me about how much the repair will cost. Does that make me "dumb" on that topic? I don't think that makes me "dumb" as a person. It may make me $1,500 poorer than I should be if the mechanic isn't honest with me about my car's need to replace its closed crankcase ventilation valve and the most efficient way to get it replaced – but that's a different matter. At some level, we end up having to have some faith in our advisors and trust in their goodwill towards us. Keep reading and we'll talk through these concerns more in Chapter 13.

Given all that, should we throw up our hands and concede defeat? I don't think we can. It's not really an option if we care about our descendants. And we can't be naïve about the task in front of us either. Knowing the difficulties created by the pre-dispositions within our humanity, and that of our descendants, forewarns and forearms us. And I think we can accomplish more than you might think. Let's press on.

ANOTHER PERSPECTIVE

There is a bit of a contrary stream of thought against the Three Generations Rule that has been gaining some momentum over the past decade or so – particularly in the family business context. To get a sampling of this, you might want to look at Do Most Family Businesses Really Fail by the Third Generation? by Josh Baron and Rob Lachenauer in the July 19, 2021 issue of the Harvard Business Review. To over summarize, there are indications that the shirtsleeves to shirtsleeves notion does not play out as starkly in family businesses and perhaps not in non-business owning families as well. A primary objection that usually accompanies this perspective is that the Three Generations Rule is too negative and too defeatist. To a point, I agree with that point of view. What almost always follows in these discussions, though, is an acknowledgement that having successful generational transfers of wealth requires hard work. On that we are fully agreed.

So, what do we do with this developing critique? As Baron and Lachenauer would say, focusing on how to achieve success is mission critical. Going further, having a hopeful, active expectation of success is also important. Where I probably land a bit differently is my sense that too many people of wealth do not fully appreciate the challenges they face and the hard work required to overcome them. While the third generation isn't "doomed to fail," we should understand that neither are they "doomed to succeed." Simply put, encouraging sustained effort to help secure successful, future generations is almost certainly of greater value than there any detriment that would accompany acknowledging and considering difficult challenges families will face in transitioning wealth.

3

The Standard
You've Set

When speaking with individuals or couples about raising their kids well in the presence of wealth, we often come to an important point in the effort early on. It's clear that the parent(s) don't want to raise spoiled children or be enablers of a "trustafarian" lifestyle. No surprise there. But how committed are they to do whatever it takes to avoid these negative outcomes?

Let me describe a scenario that comes up frequently that highlights the tension.

A married couple sold their business later in life which dramatically changed their available/spendable wealth. Prior to that point, they lived well – an upper middle-class lifestyle or maybe a titch better. Until the business was sold, outside of a comfortable salary and bonuses from time to time, most of the excess cash of the business went back into the business. They had a nice home, drove nice "company" cars, rubbed elbows with the well-to-do of their community

– but probably weren't thought of as the wealthiest family in town and they certainly didn't think of themselves in that way.

After the sale of the company, the fruits of decades of reinvestment back into the business were harvested and the after-tax proceeds of the sale were able to generate well over 5 times the prior level of income. Plus, there still was significant rental income from the real estate where the main business facility was located for at least the next five years. And no, in case you're wondering, they didn't spend 5 times what they did before. They stayed well within their means – but definitely spent more and differently.

This change in life circumstances very much brought the concern of ruining the kids with wealth experience front and center. With the youngest child in middle school and the oldest ones already established in their own careers when "the ship came in," the couple was much more concerned about ruining the youngest child with this new money than the older ones. After all, those out of the house would be less directly affected by the new wealth level. It just wouldn't be as "seen" for them as it would be for the one still at home.

When dealing with implications of this type of change, we often are brought to a central question: "If your goal is not to ruin your son/daughter with money, should you purchase that flashy car, schedule that expensive vacation, live in that neighborhood, or pursue any particular financial transaction/decision?" Most of the time, when this type of question is asked for the first time, it tends to get a bit uncomfortable in the room. It's kind of a scary question, and one that few advisors or friends in our lives would put to us. Honestly, most of us probably would rather not deal with the implications of how we would or should answer. But it is an important question. If you don't want to ruin your kids with money, are you willing to make the sacrificial life choices that will further that goal when the kids or grandkids are most vulnerable?

NOTE TO NEXT GENS

If you're someone who is/was around wealth during your "formative years," this conversation might be a bit annoying. The suggestion that a car purchase by your parents would "ruin" you could sound pretty insulting. That's not what's going on in this discussion, though.

This discussion is more about your parents than it is about you – although don't forget it's also about you in your role as a parent to your children. You have full agency over who you are and are not sentenced to being/becoming a spendthrift or unproductive adult or whatever label someone might try to give you based on what your parents did or did not do. Yet what your parents did or did not do – especially when you were in your teens and early adult years – did have some type of effect on you.

As you look both to the past and into the future, I encourage you to think about how the environment around you influenced your views on wealth and other matters. Are there stories and moments that were impactful on who you are today on these topics? What are things you need to push against and what are things that you need to embrace based on those influences?

Before we unpack the above scenario a bit further, let me be clear: this is not a book that advocates a minimalist lifestyle or intense frugality. I'm not trying to make anyone feel guilty about any particular standard of living. In fact, I personally don't see anything inherently wrong with enjoying the so-called finer things in life or necessarily any virtue in living a lifestyle way below one's means or a certain annual spend rate. What I am trying to highlight is something that you will see as a thread through just about everything in this book: the importance of identifying what's really most important to you and doing the work to align all of your choices with your self-identified, primary goals.

The question posed to our hypothetical couple is: if not ruining your kids with your money is your primary goal would you:

- Forego buying the Rolls/Lamborghini/etc. if it would make achieving that goal more difficult and drive something more modest instead?

- Choose to defer buying that amazing house on the water that you've always dreamed of for 10 or 15 years if having it sooner would make it more likely that your child would grow into a miserable person?

- Live a little less well if doing so would have a beneficial effect on your child's character and development regarding financial matters?

Questions like these are framed in a way that makes them sound easy to answer. But they're not. Regardless, you really need to know how you would honestly answer them to avoid putting any of your descendants' development in jeopardy. And if you don't like how you honestly answer them, decide if you're willing to do whatever work might be necessary to give better answers.

It's possible that early on in this book I've put you on the defensive. That may mean that we're having a new, honest conversation on tough topics. Maybe we're poking at something that needs to be poked at. If you're uncomfortable, stay with me. Even try to lean into that discomfort. This ultimately is a positive book written by someone optimistic that good people, making good decisions, motivated by love and care for their families and communities, can accomplish great things.

But before you feel off the hook with this positively worded point of view, let me emphasize how important it is for you to effectively evaluate how well you're doing in aligning your actions to your top priorities. We all want what's best, don't we? Especially when it comes to our families, we want to see our kids and grandkids and future generations grow to be moral, productive, upstanding citizens who we would be proud to know even if they weren't related to us. That objective leads many people of wealth to have moments of introspection about the values that they want to pass down to their families. Identifying and memorializing those values is certainly important — but it can't just be a laundry list of positive traits that just about anyone could put together. We have to value our values, if you will, and have the way we live our lives reflect them clearly.

I've read value statements crafted by (and for) very wealthy families that were suitable for framing. Indeed, some of them were framed. But values that don't line up with the behavior and character of those who claim to hold them dear ring hollow. Distributing them might then prove counterproductive. The project might have felt positive and meaningful for the senior generation members that had them put together. But if the next gens see it as just window dressing and empty platitudes, they won't accomplish anything long-lasting for the family.

How do you know if what you say are your values actually are your values? I've got a really simple test for you that might be helpful: look at how you spend your money and your time and you'll learn a lot about what your values are. This isn't a "religious book," but one of Jesus' sayings has some application here. He said that "where your treasure is, there your heart will be also."[7] I remember the first time I had clarity that these words were ordered the way they were. I suspect most, like me, are more likely to assume that our money follows our heart — but the more powerful pull goes the other way. We get insight into our hearts by where our money goes. It seems that time, which is another type of currency we hold, functions the same way.

Go through your spending and your calendar. What values do you see? If you say you value family, does your checkbook reflect that? If you say you value charity, how much of your time is focused on benefiting others? If you value temperance and modesty, does your spending suggest otherwise? To take it a step further, what would someone who doesn't know you discern your values to be by reviewing your checkbook and calendar? Would they say that your life and character lines up with the values you claim to espouse?

I know we all fall short of the ideals we set for ourselves. Where we do fall short, though, there can still be integrity in claiming certain values if we legitimately are working to person-

---

7   Matthew 6:21 (ESV).

ally grow towards them. I've yet to meet a perfect person, but I've certainly met people of integrity who are striving to live well. Those people are inspiring despite whatever shortcomings they may have or how far they may need to go. And their missteps from time to time do not invalidate their primary values or diminish their personal character.

When you're wealthy, it's harder to get honest insight into how you're living up to your own standards. As we discussed earlier, wealth has a distorting effect on relationships — especially with those who are impressed by it or its trappings. You probably have a number of people in your life that you're not 100% sure whether they'd be as interested in your friendship if you didn't have the wealth you have. But your checkbook and your calendar don't lie to you. Take a risk and see what they might say to you.

As sad as it may sound, some people don't want to take that risk. They like to hear what they want to hear and tolerate inauthenticity for an ego boost. If that's you, know that you're going to have a harder time protecting your children and grandchildren from the negative consequences of your wealth. The difficult task of raising solid children and grandchildren in the midst of wealth almost always requires self-awareness and likely the presence of people in your life that will say hard things to you when you need to hear them so that you can truly be self-aware. I've seen this play out poorly far too many times when things are left unsaid. Because of the impact avoidance of a full conversation can have – knowing that I'm at risk of overdoing it - let me share another scenario with you that relates to this subject.

For many years, the patriarch (could just as easily be the matriarch, so go with what suits you) of a family of wealth has been catered to by his family and by his professional advisors and preferred charitable organizations. There were a few favored advisors and friends who were treated well and allowed a bit further in to his "circle of trust." But most of those that had been brought into his life seemed overly enthusiastic in their efforts to curry his favor — and he seemed to eat it up. From the outside looking in, it appeared that the nature of the interactions between the patriarch and those in his life suggested that he had lived in this bubble of mostly false admiration and adoration for the bulk of his life.

Some cracks began to show, though, in interactions with advisors. For instance, a few of the financial advisors were on the wrong end of verbal abuse, demeaning comments, and unrealistic expectations from the patriarch. Perhaps they "took it" because they were worried about losing their jobs or "the account." Maybe they felt that accepting that behavior was actually part of the job. Regardless, the lawyer didn't see it as her place to give any personal commentary on this behavior and the accountant didn't see that side of the patriarch all that much. Accordingly, no one close enough to call him out on this behavior, nor how it didn't line up with his touted values of family and relationships, says anything. The king stays the king, and everyone continues to toast to his greatness.

In situations like these, it isn't all that uncommon to also see patriarchs and matriarchs use wealth as a tool to pit the children or grandchildren against each other or to maintain a certain level of importance in their family members' lives. The dysfunction that this wreaks within a family becomes very apparent, very quickly, after the patriarch or matriarch passes away. It is heartbreaking to see it unfold. And it can also be quite expensive if accompanied by litigation among the descendants – and it too often is. And no, there is not a level of wealth where the beneficiaries decide they are inheriting enough to forego whatever offense – real or imagined – may be present among the survivors. The dumpster that gets pulled in to be set on fire just needs to be larger the more money that's in play.

My point in describing this not uncommon scenario is to encourage you to be thoughtful as to whether people around you would say hard things to you if you needed to hear them. And if you don't have those people in your life, I hope you'll seek them out and give them space to lovingly hold you accountable to your stated priorities and values. After all, it is easier for all of us to slowly drift to the left or to the right of center when we're hearing nice and comforting things from each side of the road.

Lastly, be honest with yourself on whether you want to see things as they are or whether you have become comfortable seeing things as you want them to be. That may sound silly, but when people around you are predisposed to tell you everything is "on track" and will "turn out great," it's surprisingly easy to believe the fantasy is real. As you no doubt realize by this point in the conversation, we're going to continue to focus on the real world.

SPOUSES AS STAKEHOLDERS

Our conversation has been fairly individualized so far – but we should recognize the impact that spouses and life partners have on the process, the environment, the conversation. Basically the whole deal. They may also bring their own children from previous relationships into the family system, or have joint children with a family member creating new sibling groups and dynamics, and so on. This broadening of a family's composition can work out exceedingly well - but also can be an entry point for partiality, strife, mistrust, and a whole lot of angst after the death of the patriarch/matriarch.

When things go bad, it's easy for one side to look at the other as greedy, or manipulative, or worse. Sometimes that's exactly what's happening. More often, though, issues could have been reduced or eliminated with better communication of goals and plans and just any conversation at all. All the better if this occurs when the family member is sufficiently strong mentally.

One of the greatest gifts you can give to your family is a clear expression of your intentions and desires – especially with more complicated family structures. While there may be differences of opinion about the merits of your preferences, effective communication on potential points of stress can avoid unsolvable arguments over "perceived intentions." Further, clarity and thoughtfulness in this arena can be protective of the spouse from unfair criticism.

That said, spouses are real stakeholders in family systems – and yes, that's so for second and third (or beyond) spouses, too. While they shouldn't be bystanders in assisting in the accomplishment of a family's goals, it should be recognized that they often feel "only so in" – especially if they aren't coming from similar wealth. There may not be easy answers to intra-family dynamics with a later-introduced spouse on the scene, so if there is related friction in your family I encourage you to lean on psychologists and family system practitioners to make sure that every family member is valued fully and appropriately.

It's outside of the scope of the book to go much further on this subject, but we can at least acknowledge that incoming spouses are often treated with suspicion because everybody has a story of how an elderly individual was taken advantage of by someone swooping in and diverting all or most of that individual's wealth to themselves and ultimately their kids/families. And no question those stories are out there and too many people are victims of this type of abuse. However, these examples are not representative of most incoming spouses and shouldn't create barriers for honest, well-intentioned newcomers to be welcomed into a family.

NOTE TO IN-LAWS

To the in-laws reading this book, I see you! What a weird position you're in – at least if you don't have or come from a similar level of wealth as your spouse and your spouse's family. You probably feel hesitant or even unable to say too much about how "their" money is handled or passed down. Nevertheless, you also know that your life, your marriage, and your descendants will all be impacted by the wealth around you. And with a reduced say in how its deployed, you can find yourself in a pretty scary and uncomfortable position. Oof.

As you read this book, I'd encourage you to try not to get too caught up in the wealth around you. Rather, just as I am suggesting for the wealth-holding family overall, I suggest focusing on the personal successes of the individuals within the family and the family as a whole. You've already gotten a feel (or at least should have) that the wealth outcomes are not nearly as important as the personal outcomes. You can and should be an important contributor on the latter even if you don't have much voice on the former. You may have a tough line to walk, but if the other family members are focusing on the personal outcomes, too, there can be much success to come for all.

4

Where You're At

When I was a young attorney, I remember being asked to accompany a senior partner on a visit to one of the firm's long-standing clients. This particular client was a woman in her '80's who had just been given a grim health diagnosis and was not long for this world. Because her condition caused her to be homebound, we went to her home to execute some desired updates to her estate plan. My role was a simple one. I was going to serve as one of the witnesses to the required documents she was to sign. Despite how minimal my role was, I will never forget that visit.

We arrived at the home early in the morning and found our way to the sunlit room where we were to meet. The client couldn't have been a more gracious host. She was kind and easy to talk to. And it was clear from the outset that she was a very sharp woman. Her failing health had not impacted her mind at all.

I don't have a specific memory of what we signed or frankly all that much of our conversation. But I do remember two things as clearly as if they had happened just yesterday:

1. I remember that this woman was a beneficiary of a large trust established by her grandfather in the 1920's or 1930's. The trustees of the trust were an old-line trust company and the senior partner. Even though the estate tax exemption in the US was $600,000 at the time of this visit, and even though the trust was worth well over ten times that amount, I remember that the full trust was grandfathered from estate taxation. Millions of dollars of estate taxes would be avoided at the time of the client's death as a result of the trust structure in place. As a young associate tasked with assisting in tax minimization and avoidance for clients doing estate planning, I thought that was quite interesting and a great tax result for the family.

2. The second thing, though, is what sticks with me. In the course of our conversation a topic came up regarding a particular financial need. In that moment, the entire tenor of the interactions changed. In a flash, the mature, engaging person with whom we were considering the matters of the day seemed to have transformed and presented herself something more like a financial child. When raising her interest in a potential distribution, it seemed as though she might as well have been asking her grandfather for money. I'm not sure how else to describe it, but after she had presented her request, it felt as if she

assumed a posture of full dependence on whether the senior partner answered yes or no to the distribution.

Perhaps this isn't a fair characterization, but it seemed to play out so clearly. It was all the more noticeable and memorable because she was not a reckless spender. She wasn't someone who felt entitled to any particular level of wealth or comfort. She certainly wasn't a spoiled brat who just looked grown up. And as you probably are picking up from the way I'm telling this story, she was delightful to be around. In that moment, though, she seemed powerless. Vulnerable. In a way, even smaller, if you take my meaning. All more so than she might otherwise have been if she had had greater responsibility for her personal finances.

I may be too harsh in my assessment, and perhaps I'm not giving enough grace given how different this woman's time and experience growing up was from mine. After all, she would have been 60 or more years older than me at the time and what did I know at that point in my life? But I will say that it seems to me that most of the clients I've worked with and the people that I have interacted with of almost <u>every level of wealth</u> would prefer that their children be self-reliant even if the wealth that is or will be available to them would allow them to be otherwise. I'm assuming this would likely be your preference, as well.

When considering these matters, what stage of life you're at – or more specifically your children or grandchildren or other intended beneficiaries are at – matters a great deal. Recognizing there are tons of gradations and nuances within them, let's start by considering what I view as the three main stages of financial maturity:

Minority

There are certain legal limitations that typically apply during an individual's minority. At this stage, they cannot legally own property or care for themselves. They cannot make (at least most of) their own health care decisions. They cannot enter into contracts. Because of these and other restrictions, these types of decisions must be made by a parent or court-appointed guardian if there isn't a parent acting in the role. This means that proper planning is especially important at this stage so that, if that parent or guardian dies or becomes incapacitated, an appropriate substitute is placed in the role.

But even with these restrictions, a lot is happening during the first 18 years[8] of an individual's life. They are watching, consciously and unconsciously, to see what those around them can teach them about the world around them – including money. During this stage, it can be tough to contextualize various aspects of a parent or grandparent's wealth. But that doesn't keep a child or grandchild from taking in information and developing habits, philosophies, and perspectives that will impact their character and behavior for the rest of their lives.

---

8 Most countries use age 18 as the age of majority – but there are of course variances internationally and even within specific countries and cultural contexts. I will use this age as a proxy for the legal end of this stage – even though practically minority can extend past age 18.

Another important thing that is happening during this stage is that the individual is also developing their own agency and sense of responsibility. And it is in this area that I believe there is the most variance. How much latitude do you give to your minor child to make their own decisions? How much responsibility goes along with the decisions that they are allowed to make? Exercising and developing financial decision-making is important, but these activities tend to be most productive when there are felt consequences to the decisions made.

During minority, the parent's influence tends to reduce over time. The attitudes and experiences of peers have limited impact early on – but that influence becomes more prominent as the children move into their high school age years. As they age, children also tend to push against or question the perspectives and values of their parents on most or all things, including wealth. That's just part of growing up. Regardless, the parents' influence and example are still very important all the way through minority – including in how you push back (or don't) in a child's probing for boundaries on financial matters.

Maturation

Although not necessarily nor precisely at age 18, after childhood an individual enters into a different phase which I will refer to as the maturation phase. During this period, the individual's philosophies, objectives, morality, and general "relationship" with wealth are more moldable, but are also becoming more firm along the way. Where it starts and stops is individualized, but most people seem to reach whatever level of financial maturity that they will reach between ages 25 and 35. During this life stage, the injection of wealth without responsibility and consequences can be particularly dangerous. We know this instinctively. Just talk to any couple starting out about the potential impact on their brand-new baby if they didn't do proper planning for the wealth that they'd leave behind. They instinctively know that there is danger. Failing to put together an appropriate Will or trust would usually lead to the inheritance being fully available to the heir at age 18 when his or her guardianship would end. And the thought of putting even $50,000 or $100,000 in the hands of an 18-year-old – particularly when you don't have any clear sense of that future 18-year old's actual maturity – is scary to most.

Before moving on, I should share that I have recently been reflecting on whether the bulk of the population still reaches maturation within this 25 to 35 year range. In the past five or so years, it seems to me that this process is in part being delayed or even short-circuited by an increasing level of anxiety in the overall population. This is mostly anecdotal, and I am still unsure of what impact this societal condition might have. But if this is an issue within your family, please talk it through and consider the implications for your planning and your family. I hope to have better understanding of these matters over time but want to share this particular uncertainty in my perspective/analysis on this matter as you approach your own planning.

Maturity

At some point, the maturation process ends. The cement sets and you've got what you got. That doesn't necessarily mean that an individual is someone that would be seen as financially mature – but they will have reached whatever level of financial maturity they are likely to reach. To put it another, perhaps more crude, way: if someone is a financial screw-up at age 48, they're almost certainly going to be a financial screw-up at age 58. And at 68. People can change. For sure. But it is more the exception than the rule after a certain point. We'll talk about how to set the table for someone to be an exception to that rule later in the book.

I doubt that the above description of stages in reaching financial maturity knocked your socks off. I will say, however, it is always helpful to take a step back and see financial maturity as a process and not just an immutable state of being. Give some thought as to the desired financial maturity endpoint. What does it look like? What factors need to be present? As you consider these matters, I'd like to suggest that any individual's financial maturity is a combination of three components:

Character

A healthy, positive financial maturity will perhaps be easiest to see in an individual's character. Sometimes the analysis starts and stops at this point – but keep reading! You may define the ideal financial character differently than I do, but aspects that most would consider desirable indicators of good character include:

- Moderation and self-restraint with respect to material things.

- Discernment of the impact of today's decisions on tomorrow's experience.

- Diligence and effort in pursuing productive, positive activities.

- A sense of stewardship over personal and family wealth.

- Charity towards others.

Of course, more could (and should) be added to the list. But someone with the above characteristics would not easily be "ruined by money." Even so, I submit that it is absolutely critical that solid character on financial matters be matched in kind and degree with the next two components.

Competency

Programs driven towards preparing next gens for the inheritance that is ahead, often are geared towards what I would term financial competency. This is to be expected given that most of the creators of this programming are in the financial services industry. Make no mistake - they can be of tremendous value. While not sufficient for a successful transfer of wealth, it is critical that beneficiaries have an appropriate level of competence, or ability, to steward the wealth they might receive for them to be financially mature adults.

Financial competency can present itself as knowledge of investing or business matters, thoughtful personal spending, and the like. And the more an individual builds up their skillset in these areas, the more directly they can apply their competency to managing and contextualizing the wealth around them. However, not everyone has the interest or the aptitude for "picking stocks or bonds" or "running the family's business." Someone without these interests or aptitudes isn't necessarily any less financially mature than their brother or sister who knows how to play the game on Wall Street or in the family business' board room. Rather, the more important thing for financial competency is the ability to know your strengths and weaknesses on financial matters and how to get and manage good help where one's particular skillset or interest level isn't as strong. If you can't pick stocks well, but can pick stock pickers well, then you will still get solid results. If you can't decide what equipment to invest in on the shop floor, but know how to put trustworthy, skilled plant managers and other leaders in place who can, the results can be outstanding as well.

A bit of an aside: this may be the area that can most be outsourced of the three components of financial maturity. In fact, I see this play out frequently in the way married couples manage their own finances. Most couples that I work with seem to have a financial spouse and a non-financial spouse. Whether based on skillset, interest, or just division of the labor of running a household, one spouse tends to be much more engaged in financial matters than the other. In this sense, the non-financial spouse has outsourced their financial affairs to the financial spouse. And there's nothing wrong with that.

However, if the financial spouse dies, the non-financial spouse still needs to steward their financial affairs. Similarly, when an individual has outsourced their financial planning to someone else in the family or a financial advisor or firm, if that person becomes unavailable, the non-financial spouse still needs sufficient competency to know what to do next.

I remember this topic coming up in my own life. I had just started out my career as an estate planning attorney and was meeting with a young couple that was expecting their first child. As responsible parents-to-be, they wanted to "get a Will in place." Somewhere in our time together they asked what I had done in my own estate planning about a particular topic. At that point I hadn't done any planning. I was a bit embarrassed and decided I better do something quickly so that I could have a better answer to the "What did you do?" question that I knew would continue to come up in client meetings. When I got back to my office, I immediately got to work putting together an estate plan for my wife and me.

On a drive out to visit my wife's parents soon thereafter, I was sharing with her what I had put together for her input and approval. While the structure was easy enough for us to work through given our then modest circumstances and simple balance sheet, when I had finished describing what I had drafted for us, my wife said: "so if you were to die and this insurance money comes in, I should go to 'so-and-so' to invest the funds?" Although so-and-so was an understandable choice in that conversation, so-and-so was not the right choice for investing the insurance proceeds if the need arose. Frankly, it probably would have been a terrible choice. My wife and I needed to have a deeper and fuller conversation. And we did on the rest of our drive. To this day, the understandable, but problematic, assumption about whom my wife might have gone to for help investing the insurance proceeds continues to drive me to think about "what else do we need to cover" in every client engagement.

You may have set up yourself, your spouse, and your family with great advisors who can handle the wealth you've created with aplomb. If so, that's wonderful. But while you don't need to have your beneficiaries as engaged as you might be with those advisors, do make sure that they know them well enough and how they should engage and evaluate them (or their successors) if you're not around. Otherwise, they'll never exercise and develop the competency "muscles" that they'll need to succeed independent of you or them.

Capacity

In the past few years, I've come to appreciate this third leg of the financial maturity stool – the capacity to have and be around wealth. I see little consideration of capacity as a part of financial maturity, but a lack of capacity can overwhelm even great character and great competency. As we've been alluding to along the way, there is a stress that comes with stewarding wealth that can't entirely be quantified. And that stress hits people differently. Furthermore, that same stress can create disappointing results especially when one comes into wealth suddenly – even when sufficient financial character and competency are present.

It is not hard to find stories of lottery winners who saw their finances quickly and dramatically disappear with a corresponding disintegration of their relationships with friends and family to boot. Although it's hard to know what the percentages might really be, it is reported that a majority of NFL, NBA and MLB athletes go bankrupt or experience significant financial stresses within two to five years of retirement from their sport - a far higher rate than the population as a whole.[9]

We also see many examples of rapid diminution of wealth occurring shortly after inheritance. No doubt some of those experiences are attributable to poor character or lack of competency, but that can't explain all those results. It's hard to believe it would explain even the majority of those situations.

Instead, I submit that there is a third dynamic often at play that I label capacity. Capacity is something beyond just a comfort level with wealth. It is more akin to personal (maybe emotional or spiritual?) strength to manage the real and perceived demands that  accompany access and responsibility for a particular level of wealth. When that strength is not sufficient for the wealth present, capacity is strained and the quality of decision-making decreases.

---

9   *See, e.g., How (and Why) Athletes Go Broke,* by Pablo Torres, Sports Illustrated (March 23, 2009)

Consider, though, how some decisions made under stress that diminish wealth may on the surface seem financially counterproductive but might actually be directed toward the "productive" activity of reducing that stress. Whether consciously or unconsciously, someone without the requisite capacity to have or control a particular level of wealth might therefore find psychological reinforcement (in the form of reduced stress) when they do things that cause that wealth to fly away. Of course, there are limits and a host of other emotions and challenges that arise once the wealth is gone. These can also prove ruinous to full, future financial maturity. Either way, the surrounding wealth becomes more right-sized to the individual's level of capacity. Accordingly, these consequences and implications might make creating and building financial capacity some of the most important work you can do within your family.

What stage of maturity are your beneficiaries in? How would you rate them with respect to each of the Character, Competence and Capacity components? How is your rating impacted by the level of wealth in your family system and the knowledge of that level of wealth among your family members? How dependent are family members on you, your spouse, or someone else in the family with regard to financial matters? What impact would removal of that person from the process have on everyone else?

I realize I'm asking a lot of questions. That's intentional because, in some ways, asking the questions is part of the answer. But we'll take another, different step forward in the next part of this book.

THE UNIQUENESS OF EACH FAMILY MEMBER

The nature of this conversation leads to general statements and observations. On the individual level, though, everything plays out differently. Rarely, if ever, do all members of a generation have the same level of competency, character, and capacity. Rarely, if ever, do they have the same economic potential or interest/engagement in financial matters. Some may be really grounded and others may really struggle. Each individual therefore needs to be met where they're at and seen for who they are to have a strong management and transition of wealth within a family. I've said nothing profound here – but I hope the reminder leads to more thoughtful conversations and planning.

What often gets overlooked, though, is how planning decisions can be too driven by the extremes within a family regarding financial maturity and economic or entrepreneurial prowess. Although not universal, a strong majority of people want to treat all of their children (or grandchildren) the same. There is plenty of fodder for a discussion on equal vs. equitable in gift or inheritance planning, but the drive for equal treatment usually leads to broad application of planning appropriate for the least financially mature beneficiary and therefore overly restrictive for other family members. A more individualized approach should therefore be considered.

Families of wealth have to work extra hard to avoid economic disparities from becoming stumbling blocks and barriers within generations. If one child has an entrepreneurial spirit and a golden touch on all her projects, her siblings might feel undervalued and diminish whatever productive, but less economically rewarding, activity they might be involved in. As you consider how each child or grandchild measures up on character, competency, and capacity, you should also consider whether they are being appropriately recognized, celebrated, and supported by you and the family as a whole. This is an overly simple statement made profoundly difficult to accomplish given the variability of how society economically rewards different productive, positive pursuits.

Define the Target and the Responsibility

PART TWO

5

The Right Goals

One Sunday morning years ago, the pastor of the church I was attending asked the congregation a simple question: "What's the purpose of apple trees?" He let the question hang for a moment to let those in the room wrestle with this somewhat odd and unusual question. I remember the initial answer that came into my head: "To make apples." Perhaps that was your answer too. But he suggested a different answer: "The purpose of apple trees is to make apple trees." Now whether that's right or wrong, the implication is clear. The production of good, healthy, productive apple trees that likewise produce good, healthy, productive apple trees is a fuller measure of the success of an apple tree than how many shiny apples might be on its branches in a particular growing season.

Apple trees such as yourself, dear reader, will find it transformational to be intentional and thoughtful about prioritizing the quality of your children and grandchildren over your (or their) personal life experience. And it can be equally transformational to orient your personal planning towards generational goals instead of the inherently more limited personal goals. Wouldn't it be gratifying to see your children as good moral, upstanding, productive people raising grandchildren to be good, moral, upstanding, productive people? Unfortunately, personal planning rarely is specifically and explicitly directed towards this type of goal – which ultimately leads to less-than-ideal outcomes for future generations.

So how do you pursue a multi-generational, goals driven plan? In the preceding four chapters, we focused on the nature of the problem – the challenges associated with having wealth, how human nature works against successful outcomes, the difficulties in setting positive examples, and the process of financial maturity and danger points along each individual's development. But you don't pick up a book like this just to know the problem. You want to solve it.

The first step in solving the problem starts with you – not a solution or formula I or anyone else might suggest to you. Even though you may not know it or come into this conversation we're having believing it, defining your goals and orienting your personal planning toward the right goals is primarily your job and not the primary responsibility of your advisors. I have suggested a very broad type of goal – "producing good apple trees that produce good apple trees that produce good apple trees" – but personalizing and contextualizing that goal in a way that best fits for you and your family is hugely important. Once that important goal is set, it needs to be the overriding focus and aim of all related efforts and planning.

Advisors, of course, want to help you succeed. If they're not, they aren't the right advisors for you. At the same time, even the best-intentioned advisors can't be in full alignment with what you truly want to accomplish if you haven't communicated what your target is or don't know what that target is. This communication lapse happens all the time! And almost always completely innocently. As an example of how this plays out, let me illustrate this issue with an outline of what I'd view as the most typical way new estate planning engagements with an estate planning attorney might go:

John and Elaine MacNormal get a recommendation to an estate planning attorney from a good friend of theirs. Elaine calls in and says that she and John would like to meet because they "need a Will," although she kind of remembers their financial advisor suggesting that they might "need a Revocable Trust, too." As this is a new engagement, the attorney talks for a bit with Elaine about what information is typically helpful for putting together an estate plan, they agree on a time to meet, and ultimately get together.

John and Elaine share all the requested information, and they discuss their family situation as well as the tax and property law ramifications of this choice or that over the course of a couple of hours. At the end of their time, they agree that the lawyer should prepare an estate plan with a Revocable Trust as the primary financial vehicle. After a few weeks' time and another meeting or two, everyone is satisfied with the documents, and everything gets signed. Everyone's happy and John and Elaine get to check something off their to-do list.

Let's pause for a moment and think about how they've done so far. That initial meeting is often about one to two hours in length. Maybe a little more. Maybe a little less. In that meeting, there is some time spent on getting a handle on the client's information. Even if some of that is shared in advance, that probably takes at least 20 minutes of time. There is also a discussion of the documents themselves. Assuming the MacNormals are going through this for the first time, that probably requires at least one hour of conversation – just for describing the relevant documents, what the purpose for each might be, and what the options within each might be as well. Add in the potential need for specific conversations on tax implications, and we've probably gone past one and a half hours of time. Often that's where things stop and the lawyer and new client finish up with the logistics of when to meet next, a discussion on fees, and so on.

Along the way, there will almost certainly be discussions about goals and primary concerns. But those goals and concerns are usually expressed quite broadly and not fully contextualized to the specific project requested. You can't resolve these foundational deep matters in the 15 minutes or so of unaccounted for time in the meeting. Remember, the MacNormals said that they wanted to get their estate planning in order. And that's what they would have asked the lawyer to accomplish for them. What they didn't ask was for help defining what their primary goals or concerns were and the best way to achieve those goals and address those concerns. So even though the lawyer did the job requested in this example, and even if he or she did that job perfectly to spec, unless the MacNormals had clarity regarding their primary goals and concerns, there is no way to be 100% confident that the estate plan is in the right alignment with what's really most important to the MacNormals. Which means that it probably isn't.

Let's come at this from a different angle. Let's say the MacNormals have a $75 million combined estate and that they're facing about a $20 million estate tax bill at the surviving spouse's death.[10] Let's say the lawyer lays out a strategy that can eliminate that estate tax altogether. Sounds great, right? We want to do that plan, right?

Maybe. And here's why it's a maybe: what if getting that additional $20 million to the kids "ruins them" whereas not getting the additional amount wouldn't? If our primary goal is to raise and encourage the kids to be responsible, moral, productive, upstanding citizens, then we should abandon the $20 million tax savings strategy if it will undermine achieving our primary goal, right? As much as most people hate paying taxes, and as outlandish as paying $20 million in avoidable taxes may sound, loving parents wouldn't elevate tax savings over their children and grandchildren becoming quality people.

Now the MacNormals may still want to find ways not to pay that $20 million tax – and no doubt there will be numerous alternatives available to divert that amount to charity or to someone else. But too often conversations with advisors get out of alignment because addressing a secondary

---

10   Throughout this book, I will use very rough-cut numbers when it comes to taxes. Rates and exemptions can change significantly, so the math will almost certainly be wrong. Since I'll typically only use numbers to make a point, and given the dynamic nature of the tax system, please excuse the lack of mathematical precision.

concern – tax savings in this case – isn't considered within the context of other, higher-level goals and concerns.

The failure to tie things to an individual/couple/family's primary goals can present itself in other planning activities, too. For instance, an investment advisor might provide strategies that will significantly increase the value of the family's portfolio or an insurance agent might have the right product to create additional wealth beyond what would otherwise be achievable. While normally these results are positive, if not managed right, they can undermine the achievement of more important objectives.

NOTE TO NEXT GENS

If you're reading the MacNormals' example and place yourself in the children's generation, you probably realize that this isn't really a "kids" issue. The "over-successful trust" lands on the next generation almost always when they are adults – usually quite established adults. The risk of harm to financial maturity for you is therefore pretty low. Further, you often do not have full information or effective access to the trust – so the risk is even lower.

The dynamic is an odd one for you regardless. As you navigate through it, I encourage you to look both "above and below." In other words, as I encouraged you earlier on, think not only about the dynamics between you and your parents' generation but also what's ahead for your children and later generations. Hopefully the generation before will provide room and sufficient information for you to ready the generation after to inherit well. But if they don't, stay in the game and find positive ways to prepare your kids for their future access to family wealth. After all, any barrier to access and information is likely to be reduced after the senior generation is no longer calling the shots. And that's when things tend to get more interesting.

Let me give you another relatively common situation – at least common in the sense that most quality advisors to wealthy people have seen this play out at least a handful of times over the course of their careers: the overly successful trust. In these circumstances, an advisor may have recommended that a client make some type of gift or employ some wealth transfer technique that will reduce the client's estate for tax purposes and allow for the children, grandchildren and/or future generations to benefit from the family's wealth on a more tax efficient basis. All goes well, and then the underlying assets explode in value way beyond even the most optimistic projections. The trust could have held an interest in a family business, a private equity deal, or just a concentrated holding that grew exponentially. Regardless of the nature of the initial gift, after that increase in value occurs, the kids now have an interest in way more assets than was anticipated at the outset. In some cases, the kids might even turn out to be worth more than their parents!

Sometimes in these scenarios, everything is just fine. The parents are surprised, but happy, and the children are unharmed by the windfall. Other times, the parents are kind of upset about how things played out. They may be uncomfortable being less well off than their children – even though "they earned the wealth!" It can get worse if the children make some poor decisions with the available wealth, which becomes disheartening and discouraging to the parents. And will those decisions get worse when the parents are gone. This "over success" can lead to efforts to hide the trust's existence or scope from the beneficiaries.[11] And that

---

11 Hiding the nature and extent of a trust's holdings from its beneficiaries is becoming increasingly harder to do based on trends in the law and otherwise.

lack of transparency creates its own, mostly negative, dynamics within families.

To be clear, in these situations, I don't think the advisor has done anything wrong. In fact, they likely expertly executed a technique that the clients were very excited about at the time. But what they didn't do, because the unusual growth situation is now seen as a problem, is craft a structure that was centered on achievement of the more primary goals. The primary goal of how the kids/grandkids turn out was not a driver for the creation and design of the trust plan or its funding. If it had been, perhaps the structure would have been more responsive to the unanticipated growth of the underlying gift's value. But because the tax savings or other benefits were center stage, the misalignment eventually revealed itself with no structural response built in.

At the risk of over-doing it, let me give you another example which is much more common and familiar to advisors and clients alike in the US. The "too-big custodial account." In this situation, mom or dad, or grandma or grandpa, is told that they should use their annual exclusion gifts for the benefit of their new child or grandchild. After all, if you don't use 'em, you lose 'em.

Creating a trust for a $10,000[12] annual gift seems to be a bit of an overkill – so why not use a Uniform Transfers to Minors Act ("UTMA") account and save on the set-up costs? The account gets created and it's funded every year for 10, 15 or even 20 years. Maybe the gifts slow down when the account

---

12   For many years in the United States, the annual exclusion gift was set at $10,000 per person, per year. It is now higher based on subsequent and continuing inflation adjustments on the $10,000 baseline amount. In 2024, the amount is $18,000.

starts to grow – but it's not uncommon to see these custodial accounts worth $200,000 to $500,000 or more when that little one turns 18 and is not so little any more. It is at that point that mom or dad, grandma or grandpa, has that "oh no!" moment where they realize that come age 21 the UTMA rules say that the child or grandchild has full access to the funds. And if the child isn't ready for the money, suddenly they feel very uncomfortable.

In those cases, just like with the overly successful trust, the funders of the custodial account work hard to prevent the child or grandchild or grandchild from gaining any knowledge about the account. I've talked with people who had hidden that information from their children for decades past the 21st birthday! That's becoming harder and harder to do, and I'm not advocating for that as a solution. The point is, simple, good advice at the beginning that is not tied to primary goals can create circumstances so far out of alignment with those goals that retroactively good advice becomes bad advice.

All right. Enough on that. Let's go back to the issue of whose job it is to define the primary goals. And we've got two options: (1) you; or (2) your advisors. Let's see if we can get you off the hook first by pushing this off to your advisors.

On the one hand, let's assume you retain skilled, caring advisors. They have experience and insight about the planning process. They are experts in their defined roles, and they have seen successes and failures with other clients not only with respect to what they do, but also what other, complementary advisors do. If you have been working with them for a while, they probably have good insight into who you are and what you care about. In that sense, one or more of your advisors might have some very high positives when it comes to defining your primary goals.

Let me remind those of you in the Affluent or High Net Worth categories that goal setting is hard, but important, work. You may be tempted to try to set aside this work thinking it's only for the Ultra High Net Worth families and that advisors will only enter into these conversations with them and not with you. But it's just as important for you to get the right target set – so you just can't skip this step regardless of your wealth level.

I indicated that this book was a conversation. One way we can continue this conversation on this subject will be the expanding resources I'll maintain in response to reader and audience comments and questions at www.markshiller.com/resources/. See you there.

Should we let them run with defining the planning goals then? Well, unfortunately there are several problems with doing so. First, rarely is an advisor tasked with, and compensated for, defining primary goals. Usually, they are asked to provide advice and expertise on a specific task or specific part of the overall plan. Think back to the MacNormals above. In that example, the estate planning attorney was asked to provide a collection of documents and that engagement did not have room for a full, deep dive into primary goals and concerns. Any pursuit of those primary goals and concerns will therefore almost certainly be underinformed.

Second, there is a communication barrier if no time is devoted solely and directly to the task of discerning primary goals and concerns. Some of that barrier is whittled away the longer and closer a relationship with an advisor becomes over time – but there is always "slippage" when communication is not direct and focused on a particular matter. That slippage presents itself in incorrect assumptions and misunderstandings about a client's preferences. None of it is intentional. It just is.

Third, not every advisor has the wiring, time, or skillset to help clients discern their primary goals even when asked. If any one of those three attributes is missing there will almost certainly be a less than ideal result. And if you have an advisor who has all three – you probably still need to engage them specifically and deeply on the topic. Even with a well-equipped advisor, then, you will still have to retain at least some responsibility.

Is there any other way we can get you off the hook? Frankly, I don't think so. I didn't always think this way, but the deeper I get into these subjects with clients and deeper into the industry of wealth succession and stewardship, the more it seems that some things are best placed in the client's hands. Let me share a common scenario that probably most cemented this point of view for me:

> I begin working with a family and am excited about the great team of advisors that they've surrounded themselves with. The family's great, and the advisors are kindhearted and really skilled at what they do. No important aspect of their financial world isn't covered by someone solid.

> The team is being brought together now, though, because one of two things (maybe both) is happening: (1) the size of the estate has become, or likely soon will become, large enough that the need for planning seems very real and present; and/or (2) the kids are just becoming, or have recently

become, old enough where it seems like they should be brought into the conversation – at least on some level. All kinds of interesting ideas fly around the conference room table, and there are some decisions made.

After the meeting, everyone gets to work. The plan is updated, and implementation is moving along at just the right pace. Then the client says something like this: "would you be ok with having a meeting to explain all this to the kids?" It's not always posed to the attorney, but I know it often is when it comes to the "global plan." I also know that this question can be posed to multiple advisors in the same situation as to their areas of emphasis.

Of course, the answer is "yes." Like most advisors, I enjoy meeting the intended beneficiaries and know that a lot can get lost in translation when clients attempt to communicate trust structures or tax planning or the like. It is all very complicated after all. At the same time, the plan that is put in place has a context and should be driven towards the clients' primary goals. If the lawyer knows what those primary goals are, he or she can probably pass them along in a fuller family meeting – but what can the lawyer say about those primary goals that the client themselves shouldn't communicate to their heirs?

I can hear the objection already, though: it's too complicated for a layperson to explain all this stuff. And to be fair, when it comes to the techniques or strategies, you're probably right. In that sense, the advisors may need to provide fuller explanation of the technicalities. But, if the primary goals are yours, you should be able to explain them to your family and understand them better than anyone else. If you can state those goals simply and clearly, you also can understand and communicate why this particular, complicated strategy (that you don't need to understand at the level your legal or tax team does) is supportive and relevant to the achievement of your goals that you also can identify and communicate. And if you can't do that, how do you know if your planning is on track?

You've already taken some positive steps towards being able to communicate your planning just by reading this book. That means you've got a head start on the process already! There are some tools and plenty of food for thought on the pages that follow – so hopefully you'll feel more equipped to do your part. But the biggest thing is where we started in this chapter: define your primary goals so that you know what success looks like in your situation.

If you're ready, I'd suggest writing those primary goals down. You can always update/revise them later – but you'll have a better experience with the rest of this book if you can have some specifics to you in hand.

NEXT STEPS

After you have written down your primary goals, look over your current estate and financial plan and see if you can also write down how each component of your plan might support those goals. Perhaps it's as simple as saying things like:

- My Revocable Trust helps my assets pass more smoothly to my spouse and children so that they are taken care of in an orderly, efficient manner.

- My investment allocation is specifically targeted to produce at least what I/we will need in retirement.

- The life insurance I own will help ensure that my business will have enough liquidity to operate if something happens to me.

You might also look to go a bit deeper. Examples of doing so might include:

- The trustees I have chosen know my/our values and goals for my/our family and are equipped to mentor the beneficiaries when the time comes.

- I have collected and shared information about my financial affairs in a way that will enable a smooth transition and continued support of my loved ones.

- My spouse/children/family understand and can recite the primary goals for my estate and financial planning.

- I have directly and clearly communicated the primary goals for my estate and financial planning to my advisory team.

Your lists will be different, and it could be that you'd like to say some things now that you can't without additional work - but see how well you can do. And then, to ramp it up a bit further, identify any "supports" for each and every primary goal that you have identified. Maybe some of them will not come from the professionals on your team or require anything especially technical in nature - but there should be structures, activities and responsibilities that connect to and further each primary goal you have.

6

Own the Process

Now that we have identifiable and communicable primary goals for your estate plan, I've got an important recommendation for you. I encourage you to maintain "ownership of the process" of your personal planning. Be the general contractor of your plans. Why? Well, in some ways the reasons for you to own the process are the same as those regarding why you should be the one to define your goals. Your advisors simply aren't in a better position than you on these matters. While advisors will be an important help to get you a long way down the road, and while they will have mission critical impacts throughout, this isn't something you can fully outsource.

I'll explain what I mean more specifically about "owning the process" below, but let's consider a few factors that show why it would be unfair to expect your advisors to be in the lead position for your planning. We'll start by considering why advisors aren't in the best spot to give you and your family the sometimes hard advice that goes with developing and implementing a solid, generational wealth stewardship plan. There are more than these, but let me suggest a few reasons:

Your Advisors and Friends Are Nice People

I'm sure there are some not-so-nice people in your life, but in general, people don't want to come across as rude or harsh to those they work for or socialize with. Just about everyone is on some level a conflict avoider, too. Most people would rather not raise difficult conversations to the surface if it can be avoided. Maybe it's primarily for self-protective reasons. Maybe it's to bypass the time required to talk through things thoroughly. But there's probably a healthy portion of conflict avoidance that is part and parcel of being a decent member of society that impacts your relationships with advisors.

Years ago, I heard a story about someone who got deeply involved in politics at an early age. His role with the Democratic Party in Wisconsin put him "in the know" about how various races were going in the 1980 US elections. His position also gave him the chance to interact with the Democrat's presidential candidate that year: Jimmy Carter. Apparently, the outlook for Carter in Wisconsin was bleak at the time. Even so, this young man had ideas that he strongly felt would reach the local electorate and perhaps turn the tide. For weeks he thoughtfully considered what he might say to the President when he ultimately came to visit the party's Wisconsin campaign team.

The day finally came, and President Carter entered a room filled with the enthusiastic, cheese-loving party faithful. As he made his way through the room, he came to this young man. Upon being introduced and told of the role he had in the election effort, the then candidate asked a simple question: "How are things looking for us this November in Wisconsin?" There couldn't have been a more open door for him to share all the data he'd sifted through and analyzed over the past weeks and months. It was a natural invitation to share his thoughtfully developed strategies to turn away the expected Reagan victory – at least in Wisconsin. What did he say? Well, he froze. He could not bring himself to say what a moment earlier he was bursting at the seams to say. In the presence of the man, he could muster nothing more than, "Just fine, sir." And with that, the President thanked him, shook his hand, and walked over to the next person with no new, helpful information out of that exchange.

I'm not suggesting that the election would have turned out differently if this young man had spoken up. Not at all. I share this story because it illustrates that there is an inherent bias to tell people of wealth, power, and fame what they want to hear – even when you have the best and most helpful of intentions towards that person. Ultimately, when you are face-to-face with someone, especially someone you like, love or respect, it's hard to say hard things to them. And it's that much tougher to do so when your relationship is only so deep or just beginning.

Your Advisors Like Having You as Clients

This book is not a deep dive into the financial services industry – maybe I'll tackle that another time if there's an interest. That said, while there are some bad apples out there, in my experience, most advisors want to do right by their clients. But that doesn't mean they're in a strong enough personal financial position, or are personally comfortable enough, to say the tough things their clients might need to hear as doing so could also end up getting them fired. Of course, not everyone's motives are pure, but let's consider how things might progress with a well-meaning advisor/client relationship. Here's a typical lifecycle of many advisor-client relationships:

1. At the beginning, almost every advisor associated with an individual, couple or a family's wealth starts with a discovery process. They need to get to know you, right? So they ask questions, gather data, and spend time with you, all with the end goal of setting the stage for a long, positive, mutually satisfying relationship. This isn't a great set up for a (potential) advisor to tell you that you're not dealing with your kids/grandkids in the right way, is it? Besides, they're just getting to know you. It'd be too early to make those kinds of judgments. Right?

2. Assuming you move forward and hire the advisor, he or she wants to put their best foot forward and solidify the strength of your relationship. Until the cement sets on that, it'd be a bit more of a risk than it's worth for the advisor to suggest that you're not doing a great job with your kids/grandkid on wealth matters or otherwise. Don't you agree? And heck, they probably don't know enough at this stage to have any authority on the topic.

3. After you've passed the honeymoon stage and a bit of time has gone by, your once new advisor now knows

you well. A lot of times they may only know your kids and grandkids through you, but let's say they now know your family well, too. What might cause a conversation to start with a question like "don't you think you could be doing a better job with your kids/grandkids on X or Y?" Maybe a crisis in the family, but otherwise, it's no small thing to bring up such a serious topic. And heck, they probably can come up with any number of reasons why they could be off base or out of line if they brought it up.

4. Now you've worked together for 5, 10, 15 or more years. You're friendly with each other and appreciate the working relationship. You're a good person, and your advisor really likes and respects you. Why rock the boat and bring up your potential/actual deficiencies in year 9? And why now? And if not at that point, why ever? Besides, when the wealth changes hands, someone else will probably be involved and the kids/grandkids will be that much more mature at that point. It'll all take care of itself, right?

It might not go the way I've laid it out above. But I do think this is a fairly typical path for a long-term relationship with a financial advisor, accountant, attorney, and the like to go. And no one's done anything wrong by keeping their mouth shut. But there's one other very important reason why your advisors aren't going to tell you that you're making errors in how you're planning for the impact of your wealth on your ultimate beneficiaries.

You Didn't Ask Them

You probably didn't ask your advisors to tell you whether you're approaching the stewardship of your wealth across generations properly. Even if you wanted this type of advice, few individuals, couples, or families hire someone with the specific task of giving focused direction and perspective on how to leave the most positive impact on your family and your community. Consider:

- You ask financial and investment advisors to provide you with investment advice and you pay them to do so.

- You ask your CPA to provide you with tax planning and compliance advice and you pay them to do so.

- You ask your attorneys to advise you on the structure of your estate plan and to create and implement the legal structures and documents needed and you pay them to do so.

- You ask your insurance advisor for help matching and designing an insurance product to meet an insurance-related need and you pay them to do so.

Of course, any one of the above (and other categories of advisors not listed above) may offer additional services that address legacy topics. And if they do, that's fantastic! But it's not usually the primary thing you retain that advisor for. That can impact the advice you might get for a variety of reasons including: the depth of relationship with the legacy advisor, shyness about raising tough topics that might impact the primary - from a revenue standpoint - advisory arrangements, and the like.

This might seem obvious to you. Perhaps you can't imagine not "owning the process." At the same time, many people are drawn to the idea of hiring an advisor who can take it and run with it. In the US, that person might identify themselves as serving as the "quarterback" for you

> Of course, you could ask your advisors for help on these topics. Some will be happy to engage in the conversation, some might be unsure about it. They might also be uncertain as to how to charge for their advice if the project becomes intensive. That's kind of its own topic that I'll address more at www.markshiller. com/resources/ - but it'd be great for you to open the door to what hopefully will be more focused and productive connections with your key advisors.

and your family. Basically, that means that that advisor will take responsibility for establishing what they feel needs to be done and making sure that everything is accomplished. Good idea? Bad idea? Of course, as with most things, it depends.

On the one hand, having a quarterback to make sure that each person is doing what they are supposed to be doing in a coordinated fashion can be great. Sometimes really great. If that advisor is sophisticated and organized enough, they can be tremendously helpful in keeping things moving forward and on task. If they're not, that's another story – but let's assume that this advisor is sufficiently sophisticated and organized. Does that change who should have primary ownership of the process?

I don't think so for a few reasons:

First, the quarterback can easily drift into his or her own interpretation of the goals or imperfectly understand your primary goals. If you're going to use them, make sure you're still the head coach calling the plays and evaluating the quarterback's performance.[13]

Second, the difficulty of the task of successful wealth transfers makes outsourcing the tough stuff you know you should keep on your plate almost too tempting. Having a willing quarterback on the job makes it too easy for you to push off an item or two from your punch list to that of the quarterback and never ask for it back.

Third, most of the time the quarterback is not paid to be a quarterback in a family wealth situation. They're usually paid for some other service – maybe it's based on assets under management, services provided more broadly, sometimes on commissions on financial products. Whatever it is, they're still compensated for something other than quarterbacking services. And this disconnect between role and compensation will almost inevitably have some consequence. Not necessarily a terribly negative consequence. But it will have a consequence that you at least need to think through and account for in your work together.

The bottom line of this discussion is that I'm not against having someone in a coordinating role under most circumstances. It's just that when you have someone in that role you will have to account for the dynamics that go along with that role and make sure that tasks are chosen and implemented properly and in accordance with your overarching goals and objectives.

With all that said, I would be remiss if I didn't discuss where I'm very negative on having a third-party quarterback/coordina-

---

13   Am I doing too much sports analogy talk yet? I try not to overdo it, but I feel trapped by how often I hear the term "quarterback" on this subject.

tor: whenever that third-party jockeys for the position in order to have what some advisors might term "client control." I really hate hearing that term. No advisor should have any level of control over their clients or anyone else for that matter. But I've heard advisors use the term when the clients aren't in the room, and I've witnessed that mindset in action. Almost all the time it comes from a place of insecurity from the advisor seeking to be in charge. And insecurity in an advisor married with "control" can be quite dangerous. Let me describe how this might play out in real life.

A business-owning couple has been doing well financially. They've determined that none of the kids are going to get involved in the business and it's time to sell. All their years of sacrifice for the growth of the business will pay off handsomely, but the thought of going from day-by-day control over their financial holdings to putting it all into the market and someone else's hands sounds scary. But it's time. They need to sell, and there's no better time than the present to get to work on their post-business owning world.

With no full advisory team in place – after all, almost all of the cash went back into the business, so there was no need for a financial advisor – the clients receive a referral to someone at Brady, Unitas, & Montana. They hadn't heard of the firm, but they understand that they do [you decide the primary service provided] and this new guy, Patrick, seems very eager. In fact, he's arranged for a 360 review of everything and will come back with recommendations on all aspects of the plan.

All the relevant information is exchanged, Patrick pulls it altogether, and gets together with the couple. As they're getting started, he slides a thick binder full of graphs, numbers, and strategies across the table. The couple is of course impressed and enthusiastically tell Patrick to go for it on the whole plan.

What happens next is usually the most interesting. It's time to gather the team. But there isn't a team in place just yet. No matter, Patrick will take care of that, too. And when they gather to discuss the plan, the team appears. Assembled and eager to help. Everyone loves the plan. Everyone gets to work. And soon enough, it's done.

Good ending? It's probably not a bad ending. The plan might also be just fine. But here's the deal: Patrick and his team better be the smartest people in the room and have engaged enough sophistication on the areas where they brought in others outside of their firm to get the "best plan." They also should have the integrity and humility to know where they don't have the best solution and refer things out accordingly. More importantly, if the clients buy the whole package, they also need to rely on Patrick to tie everything back to the family's most important goals. And only the best purveyors of the whole package make sure that those primary goals are the primary drivers.

I will admit that I tend to chase the ideal without giving enough credit to achieving the "not bad." You may balance those scales differently than I – and you might make the better call on balancing these considerations than me. At the same time, when a situation isn't ideal, I also want to make sure there isn't something else going on that turns the achieved "not bad" into something exploitative or that will lead to future problems. In the hypothetical situation I described above, this can play out by the Patrick character asserting "client control" by keeping the advisory world too small given the circumstances and insulating the clients from other options, notions, and ideas that might be better than the best he could come up with. Generally, with the conscious or unconscious goal of the advisor's maintenance of the relationship and associated fees.

By owning the process, and competently managing who you bring around the table, you do more than keep your goals front and center. You also keep everyone accountable to serving you and your family at the level of service and proficiency that you need. And ultimately, good advisors will want that, too.

NEXT STEPS

Consider your estate and financial plan. How much of it would you say was driven by you and how much by your advisors? Is there someone who might be the chief architect of the plan on the scene? Is that someone someone other than you? Has either situation been comfortable or uncomfortable? After reading this chapter, do you feel differently than you did before?

Relatedly, you might find it helpful to consider what aspects you are least comfortable with or knowledgeable about with respect to your planning. While getting more educated and conversant in these matters might be worthwhile, it's also a good idea to understand where your weak points are. You might even make a list of them. Armed with this knowledge, though, you should prepare yourself to stay engaged in future aspects of your planning even in aspects where you're least comfortable.

Remember, you are the client and have the greatest interest in keeping your goals center-stage. Don't underestimate the importance or value of maintaining that focus in all aspects of your plan or let discomfort with any particular part of your planning lead you to pull back from owning the process.

CONVERSATION OPENERS TO OWN THE PROCESS

You may have come up with a lot of your own thoughts and strategies to maintain ownership of your planning process. If so, I'd love to hear what you came up with! But if you're stuck on how to make "owning the process" real for your situation, here are a few ways that might open the door to great conversations with your advisors and family:

- Tell each advisor that's important to you what your primary goals are. After doing so, simply ask, "how does our work together further these goals?" Follow up with the question: "is there a way that it might work against my goals?"

- Engage your advisors on how things might look if your net worth grows significantly. Maybe you won't invest in additional work at the moment to address that possibility currently, but you might gain some ideas to hold in your back pocket if things start to go up in value more than expected.

- Do the same exercise regarding what happens if things go significantly down in value.

- Ask each advisor whether they would benefit from connecting with another advisor on specific points. Perhaps ask them to communicate with that other advisor regarding how their work ties to your primary goals as a way to expand the conversation within your fuller advisory team.

- If you have some wise friends in your life that have considered these topics, reach out to them and compare notes on how each of you have integrated your primary goals into your planning.

- This might be a struggle, but try to talk through how your planning ties to primary goals with your family. If it doesn't work out well in your first attempt, go back to your advisors for clarification and then try again with family. Resist the temptation to "phone a friend" and turn things over to that advisor and instead use the "struggle" to push everyone – including your advisors – towards greater clarity and alignment in your planning.

7

Get Over Yourself

Most engagements regarding the implications of wealth transfer start with the current members of the senior generation.[14] They've got the money, after all. They most feel the weight of the problems and responsibility for the outcome. They buy books like these. They talk about their concerns with their advisors – or at least want to. They usually control what happens next with the assets. And they generally control who gets paid to be involved in the process. So it makes sense that they would be the focal point of wealth transfer planning and activity. But this also has its own distorting effect on the achievement of

---

14   We haven't really discussed how I'm using generational assignments and labels. Yet, I recognize that it can sometimes be confusing. For instance, referring to the "senior generation" could mean the first generation to create the wealth or perhaps the generation that currently has the greatest control over family wealth at the moment. They might be one in the same, but more often I will be primarily referring to the latter situation. In addition, keep in mind that numerical generational assignments are also relative. So while Gen 1 (this is the format I'll use for referring to Generation 1, etc.) represents the parents of Gen 2 and grandparents of Gen 3, they also were in the position of being children or grandchildren at one point, too. Hopefully you'll be able to keep track of who's who and in what position from here on out. Keep a notepad handy if it helps!

goals accomplished generationally. After all, it is the long-term health and productivity of the third-generation apple tree and its progeny and not the one producing apples today that will reveal whether we succeeded or not.

Sometimes (I think often) the importance of those at the center of the process is overstated to stroke the egos of the current wealth holders. Maybe it's good business for the advisory world to do so. If it is, then it makes sense for advisors to structure wealth transfer engagements to maximize how good the senior generation feels at the end. The idea of legacy then begins to feel like a personal, individual endeavor. But here's the thing: your legacy plays out long after you're gone. And if you're the current, primary holder of the family wealth, in many ways, you have the least ability to secure the achievement of multi-generational legacy goals that you might have. There's no doubt that you can and should have a significant impact. There's no question that you can do a lot of good to foster future successes. But ultimately, your kids and grandkids will have more to say about how they and their offspring will "turn out" and what your legacy produces than you will.

Not too long ago, I had a conversation with my oldest son and his wife. On the call, my son was nice enough to say that my wife (and his mom) and I did a good job raising them. I think we certainly did alright, and I'm very proud of each of my children – but I also strongly believe that each child has the bigger claim to whatever successes they've had or will have. My wife and I encouraged them to have a good work ethic, but we didn't "make them" have a good work ethic. Their choice to work hard or not was the determiner of whether our encouragement worked or didn't work. We may have encouraged them to be careful with their finances and spending, but eventually and early on their choices became their choices. In these and other areas, their decisions (and not ours) determined their success and revealed their character.

Perhaps this sounds like splitting hairs or being too dismissive of the positive impact a parent might have on their children – but I don't think so. While we let the thought about how much good a parent can "make happen" sit for a moment, let's consider the other side of the coin: how much negative impact can a parent have. I submit that greater focus and concern should be on the negative than on the positive for this topic. Here are a few situations where parents can do harm that lead me to this point of view:

The Hard Driver Parent

Acknowledging that there may be plenty of cultural or personal choices as to how to parent well, there is a type of parenting where the parent focuses significant energy into "making" their child a success. It could be the "Hollywood Mom" pushing to get her child to land this role or that so they can be the next big star. Or the parent who sacrifices time and money to see their child excel at sports. We also see this in academics and other talents and skills that tend to be rewarded monetarily or otherwise. While it's laudable to make sacrifices for the betterment of your children, at some point it can become dysfunctional and the parent is more of a puppet master than parent.

A classic example of this that comes to mind is the story of Marvin Marinovich, father of Todd Marinovich. Marv, as he was known, is infamous for his overwhelming drive to see his son become a professional athlete. According to the article, *Bred to Be a Superstar,* by Douglas S. Looney in the February 22, 1988 edition of Sports Illustrated, Todd was considered "America's first test-tube athlete." Marv began conditioning his son for future athletic prowess as early as one month old by stretching out his hamstrings. He famously restricted his son's diet to avoid all sugar and refined, white flour. His whole childhood was driven toward athletic achievement.

And it worked. For a while. Todd set records out of high school. He played for the University of Southern California – one of the premier college football programs in the United States. And he ultimately became a first-round pick of the Los Angeles Raiders in the National Football League. But the pressure and intensity of the curated cradle to NFL stadium experience, and no doubt a healthy portion of Marv's abusiveness and abrasiveness towards Todd, his family and really to almost everyone around him, contributed to Todd's ultimate fall into drug and alcohol addiction. His professional football career evaporated quickly and Todd is likely working on overcoming his past to this day.

None of us knows the whole story – and no doubt there is much that we don't know that would impact the lessons we might draw from this over-the-top example of hard-driving parenting. But placing too much weight on the success of your children typically does have a counterproductive effect that bubbles to the surface eventually. And it would seem that the greater the emphasis on future "success," the more likely the ending is eventually poor.

The Long Shadow

Many times, the person at the center of a wealth transfer discussion has a notable personal drive and skillset that led to a certain level of success financially or otherwise. Even if it was just dumb luck, though, whatever might have been achieved is typically accompanied by praise and adulation for the wealth creator. That success can not only create significant expectations for the descendants that has its own effect but might lead the senior generation individual to consciously or subconsciously project expectations on the next gens to show "enough success" to validate their own. These later-in-life expectations can be disconcerting and confusing to those who hadn't been told they were expected to be validators of their parent or grandparent's earlier in life successes.

The Doubter

Often coupled with the Long Shadow is the Doubter – the parent who either explicitly or implicitly doesn't think that their child or grandchild will ever measure up or make good decisions. And sometimes the decision making of a particular individual might reveal them to be pretty lousy in this area or that. But what if the level of doubt makes poor decision-making more likely? Especially if that doubt is expressed at a time when character is being formed?

There is a Warren Buffett quote that is often brought up when it comes to not ruining kids with money:

I want to give my kids enough so that they could feel that they could do anything, but not so much that they could do nothing.

There is a simplicity to the language used, and the balance inherent in the quote has its own kind of beauty. But there also might be an underlying assumption within that sentiment: there is a certain level of wealth that the kids can't handle. And given the statements made by Mr. Buffett regarding his own plans, there is at least an implication that the level of wealth (the enough/not too much level) is a small fraction of the wealth that he currently has.

I don't know Warren Buffett or his family, so I'm just parsing the language and not making any commentary on the Bufetts' choices or thoughtfulness on the topic. What I am saying, though, is that if someone grabs onto that quote as a guidepost for their own planning, they should also consider the underlying assumptions that come with the quote and a number of other questions. If that's you, let me give you a few of those questions to work through:

What level of wealth do I think would cause my children/grandchildren to think they could do nothing?

If they had that level of wealth, would they do nothing? If so, why might that be?

If that level of wealth I think my children or grandchildren could handle is less than the wealth I have, why isn't the level of wealth I have too much for me?

I get that it probably seems foolish for a no name like me to be critical of a well-known and oft quoted pearl of wisdom from Warren Buffett. At the same time, it is so easy to blow by the implications of the answers to the above questions – particularly the last one. Because if you think your heirs can't handle wealth as well as you, you have to think long and hard about what that might say about you and what it might say about your heirs.

In the above and other negative parenting circumstances, there is a common thread – the parent is at the center and the child's performance or choices are viewed as proxies for the parent's successes or failures. Healthier parenting would see the child thriving as its own and sufficient goal. To reflect back on an earlier discussion, stepping back and seeing an orchard of strong, healthy apple trees should be far more rewarding than having a nice bowl of shiny apples on the kitchen table.

So here's my main advice for you in light of the above discussion: get over yourself. Since you can't force success on the next generations, don't try to force success on the next generation. Be honest whether you might be projecting doubt as to the capacity of your children and grandchildren to make good life choices and whether that's unfair or counterproductive. And if you've made wealth transfer activity too much about you, stop it. Maybe no one will tell you it's been too much about you, but it'll be much easier on you and others if you arrive at the conclusion yourself.

For some of you, the above advice is "course correction" advice. For others, you might have no idea what I'm talking about. You aren't making it all about you, you say, and you're not that kind of person. And many of the people of wealth I interact with on these topics are that way, too. At the same time, the process has made it all about them in many, often subtle, ways. Even if you don't need to course correct how you view the world or the process of dealing with a wealth transition, the process needs to be managed in a way that doesn't over-emphasize your role. In a weird way, then, my advice to get over yourself is almost as valid and important for those that "don't need it."

Before moving on to the next topic, let me bring up one more thing. Even within families, the desire to serve the legacy of even the most beloved ancestor has its limits if the ancestor's goals don't line up with the goals of the next generations. Ancestors often don't see the collapse in apparent family unity coming. But after death, or in the event of significantly diminished capacity, the unresolved "fights in the sandbox" that siblings had as children tend to flare back up. The affront one child might feel regarding another's lack of involvement in the ancestor's care or personal life, or his or her interest in the family business, or just about any type of actual or perceived deficiency is brought to the fore. Now without the senior generation member's presence to tamp down the heat of the long-suppressed and smoldering disagreements. The proxy for these offenses is almost always "the money." At this point, the quiet experienced by the ancestor during life proves not to be indicative of peace and harmony within the family, but rather the calm before the storm.

A blow up after a patriarch or matriarch's death is a very familiar story – and even the plot of many books and movies. I suspect most readers have seen it play out in their family or in a family of someone close to them. While these awful stories would seem to be motivation for not "kicking the can down the road" on good planning, they also show one of two things about many patriarchs or matriarchs: (1) they are terrible at anticipating that things will go poorly after they pass; or (2) they prefer the quiet over the effort required to avoid a poor experience. I

> This issue of family strife surfacing after the death of a senior generation member rears its ugly head seemingly without regard to wealth levels. You're fooling yourself if you think this only shows up in the wealthiest families. If you and your family are in the so-called Mass Affluent category, do not discount the possibility of future battles over family wealth.

suspect it's usually the latter given our propensity as humans to put off hard things and conflict. Regardless, another way to get over yourself is to buck up and do the necessary work involved, even when unpleasant, to address things as they are and not delude yourself that it'll all work out when we have no evidence (other than quiet) to suggest it will.

NEXT STEPS

Here are some thoughts as to what "getting over yourself" looks like in practice:

1. You actively look for ways to bring the next generations into the conversation instead of insisting on keeping them in the dark.

2. You learn to trust each generation with the responsibility and the opportunity to succeed in stewarding the following generation's success.

3. Conversations with your advisors are seasoned with more and more aspects of the next generation's lives and experiences than your own.

4. The job of managing wealth transition moves from being "your job" to "our job."

5. You don't like all the decisions made, but see how they fit into more global, family-wide goals.

6. Your children/grandchildren have the time to grow into their roles, even if they stumble a bit out of the chute.

7. Your opinion and perspective are sought out more than they are offered unsolicited to the next generation.

Many of the above imply that "the kids" have reached a point of maturity where it's appropriate to include them in the process. When that might be and what that looks like is a later discussion in this book. Regardless, reflecting on questions like those above will help you visualize what it might look like for your full family to have ownership of the multi-generational goals we've been discussing. If you're not there yet, do your best to project out and anticipate future input and involvement of future generations.

Write down your perception of where things stand on the above 7 points. Does the sum total of your answers suggest that you're too center stage – intentionally or unintentionally? If so, think through how you might need to get over yourself.

8

Giving Over Success

In the previous chapter, I suggested that senior generation members are limited in the positive effect they can have on multi-generational goals such as the goal of raising good, financially mature kids who raise good, financially mature grandkids. Later in the book I will suggest a number of things you can do to increase the positive effect you can have if you're in the senior generation – but still, there are limits. Perhaps the most positive thing you can do – assuming you've gotten over yourself -- is what I term "Giving Over Success." Let's dig into that next, because I think you'll find it adds color to almost everything else we'll cover in this book.

You'll recall our discussion on how the Three Generations Rule proverbs suggest a universal, hardwired, human nature concern. But it's also a picture of a failed estate plan. After all, who would view building up a massive amount of wealth only to see it dissipate into insignificance by the time it gets to their grandchildren as a win? Keep that type of failure in mind as we consider another question that strikes me as a natural follow up to the Three Generations Rule: why it isn't shirtsleeves to shirtsleeves in two generations? Let me suggest a few reasons why failure doesn't normally occur in Generation 2.

Timing for Gen 2

When the senior generation dies and leaves their wealth behind, the second generation is generally in their 50's, 60's and 70's.[15] I've seen people inherit in their 80's, too. Just a short time ago before this book will be published, my grandfather passed away at 98 ½ years of age. He survived my grandmother by a few years, so he was the surviving parent for my mother and her two brothers. We were all grateful for his (and my grandmother's) long life and presence in our lives, but that also meant that my mother's inheritance occurred at age 77 – at a point in her life where the funds received were not going to have any real impact on my mother's character or financial life given that both were long established independent of any inheritance.

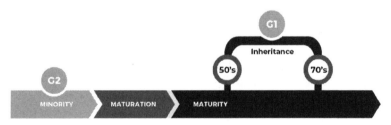

---

15   Over the past 100 to 150 years across the globe we have seen significant increases in life expectancy. In the United States, for instance, life expectancy has essentially doubled from about 40 in the mid- to late 1800's to almost 80 today. And with the fastest growing demographic in the developing world often being those in their 90's or above, we will increasingly see inheritances happening when the second generation is in their 80's. This will no doubt create a need to adjust much of our thinking on wealth transfer planning, especially if longer lifespans are not accompanied by later retirements.

While there are plenty of 70-somethings who can cause their share of damage with extra money in their pockets, in general, at this stage, you've lived a certain lifestyle and are not likely to make radically different choices regarding spending – at least on yourself – or your finances more broadly in the years to follow. The energy and effort that's required to "blow an inheritance" is simply reduced at this stage of life.

Knowledge for Gen 2

Assuming that there hadn't been complete transparency on the level of wealth until late in life, the children's generation likely had an inaccurate and incomplete understanding of the wealth available to the senior generation. Generally, children of wealthy parents significantly underestimate the wealth of their parents. They usually assume a net worth that is 1/3, 1/4, or even 1/5 or lower than what it actually is. Why? I don't think it's because they're bad guessers. In fact, I tend to think they're pretty good guessers when you consider that they base their guesses on the best available information – how mom and dad spend money. And if mom and dad live below their means -- as most of my friends and clients of means seem to do, anyway – the "low" guesses make sense.

When coupled with the later-in-life timing of inheritances, if the guesses as to their parents' wealth are proved to be wrong when the parents are in their 50's, 60's or 70's, the life choices of the children in the 20's, 30's and 40's – the most formative period – were likely less impacted negatively. There certainly can and will be an impact to ultimately discovering the significantly greater wealth – but the magnifying effect of high wealth (or the expectation of receiving high wealth) is muted at the most critical juncture.

Expectations for Gen 2

The later the transfer of wealth occurs, the more likely it is that the next generation hadn't been banking on it coming to them any time soon. There may be a head knowledge that it'll come one day – but especially in current times, if a parent is reasonably healthy in their 70's, it is increasingly reasonable to expect them to live until their 90's or 100's. If that's so, that 60- or 70-something will probably be going about their financial decision-making without a specific expectation of future, inherited wealth driving their decision-making.

Of course, there are significant exceptions to all of the above. Bad results don't always "skip a generation." There are children who overspend waiting for mom and dad to feel sorry for their financial straits and bail them out – or more often waiting for the inheritance that will solve their bad financial decisions. There are families where wealth is used manipulatively or co-dependently between Gen 1 and Gen 2. Sometimes there were enough wealth flows in the 20's, 30's or 40's that led to reduced incentive or energy in Gen 2 to dig in and establish strong financial independence from Gen 1. Further, how these issues land on individual members of Gen 2 can vary quite a bit – which might also add to the dynamic of resentment, suspicion, and other disconnects between siblings.

These and other analogous situations are all bad results in Gen 2. Yet it might also be fair to characterize them as requiring some break from the typical interactions between Gen 1 and Gen 2 regarding wealth or that there is some unhealthiness regarding wealth in the family system. Let me expand on what I mean by typical and/or healthy:

- Wealth flowing from parents to children might be generous, but not at the level that would give the children the ability or desire to abandon a pursuit of financial independence.

- If parents perceive that their children are becoming too or fully dependent on their financial largess, they would pull back on gifts and other provisions.

- Self-aware children might find it difficult to do so, but in the healthiest situations they will pull themselves back from over-reliance on their parents' wealth.

In addition to all this, children "feel" the wealth of their parents differently than grandchildren do. There are natural distinctions between relationships between parent and child and grandparent and grandchild, of course. But there is also the matter of time. The grandchildren are on a parallel track to their parents – but roughly 30 years behind. Although on the one hand, they might find themselves in a similar position to the children in terms of when they might inherit or what their life experiences might be, it is necessarily a different experience for the younger generation when the wealth is created one or more generations prior to their parents' generation.

Timing for Gen 3

As we observed a little bit ago, the third generation is most likely be in their 20's, 30's and 40's when their parent or parents would inherit from the prior/grandparents' generation. At that stage of life, the third generation hasn't likely raised their own children to adulthood, haven't had full careers, are more likely to be experiencing financial pressures that accompany earlier life stages, etc. They haven't necessarily gotten to full financial maturity either. Which means they haven't had the amount of "in adulthood" time their parents had to wrestle with the issues and challenges that accompany wealth within a family system. That makes the grandchildren more vulnerable not only to the impact of an inheritance but also to the impact of the knowledge of a future inheritance.

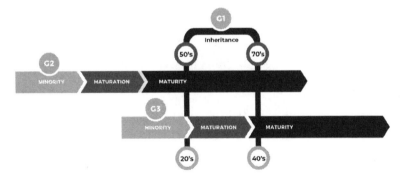

Knowledge for Gen 3

While the second generation usually doesn't know the full extent of what their inheritance will be until later in life, the third generation typically has greater awareness regarding family wealth much earlier. A good deal of this can be attributed to the freer flow of information that usually comes from their parents who may have preferred that they themselves had received more information earlier on. It may also be due to a need for the inheritors in Gen 2 to process the inheritance experience with someone they can feel safe with – like their adult children in Gen 3. These behaviors tend to be more pronounced the more tight-lipped the first generation had been until the wealth transfer does in fact happen. We've covered this already, but when the inheritors discover that the family's wealth is much greater than they would have guessed (again, as is usually the case), the excess is more likely to be seen as found money. The recipients are surprised – in most ways likely pleasantly so. But they may also find it unsettling and difficult to take in - and accordingly more likely to lead to information regarding the inheritance to leak out.

This is simply stated, but I believe it to be a profoundly impactful matter. The senior generation worries a lot about the flow of information to the child's generation when what they should really be worried about is the flow of information from the child's generation to the grandchild's generation – most often occurring at a point in time when they have zero ability to affect what is shared downstream. And whatever hesitation they might have regarding sharing the information with their children, it must be counterbalanced with how not sharing the information will lead to poorer information flow and overall experience a generation down.

NOTE TO NEXT GENS

Consider how you would approach a good-sized inheritance coming to you right at the time when you have a big expenditure coming up. Maybe you need to replace your car or your oldest child is going to college. Something like that. Now that you have that in mind, think about how you would approach that expenditure if your inheritance were fully in your control or if it were subject to someone else's control.

Your answer may tell you a fair amount about spendability for you. Although I have an admittedly limited dataset to draw from on this subject, I have seen this scenario play out multiple times. And recipients who don't have control tend to seek greater disbursements from the inherited funds than those with control.

The results are more even when there has been good discussion in advance of the inheritance. But when that hasn't happened, beneficiaries' increased desire to spend is notable. As one beneficiary in that situation observed, "I had wanted to get more out of the trust when someone else was in charge, but thought differently after I saw the funds as my own." Spending less is not necessarily the point. Rather, the closer consistency with personal and family values when one thinks like an owner or steward is what's important.

Whatever inheritance might be available or coming to you, and whatever structure may be in place regarding the access and control of the wealth you might have, I encourage you to make any personal financial decision as an owner and steward would. This will be all the more important for you to take this on if your parents and grandparents haven't engaged with you on these matters.

Expectations for Gen 3

Remember that children and young adults who are not directly educated on these matters make their judgments based on behavior. We therefore should consider what they more likely will see occur if their parents receive a significant inheritance. Even if to the outside observer the second generation doesn't over-spend based on the additional resources available, the second generation usually has some additional expenditure or makes some notable change in behavior. Maybe it's a house upgrade, or a vacation property, or a new/better car, or better vacations, etc. If the wealth level is high enough, one or two splurges in the first year or two is not unusual. And generally not inappropriate either. However, the grandchildren's generation most likely sees that increased wealth leads to additional expenditures more quickly than their parents' generation would see. For the grandchildren, the transaction seems to unfold in just a year or two. For the parents, the transaction is seen more as a generational or once in a lifetime event.

Spendability for Gen 3

We should also account for how inherited wealth is generally seen as more spendable than personally earned wealth. This may seem an odd analogy – particularly if you don't live in a climate where you experience winter the way I have all my life – but consider the experience of pulling out your winter coat when the temperature starts to dip and finding a $20 bill in one of the pockets. This found $20 gets spent much more freely than the $20 you had in your wallet the whole time. There's no difference in the characteristics of that $20 bill, other than how it "showed up." And there's nothing different about inherited money vs. money in the inheritor's bank account – but it feels different because of how it shows up. And that difference manifests itself in poorer retirement planning, freer spending, and a more cavalier attitude towards wealth. In other words, it is more likely to lead to wearing shirtsleeves.

In the context of our discussion, the grandchildren will experience their parents' increased spendability with the funds that their parents in Gen 2 never experienced from Gen 1. Gen 1 may have lived well, but they typically tend and grow the funds with the seriousness that comes along with having been responsible for it for sometimes well over 50 years. Without that experience, any stewardship attitude will tend to degrade when the assets flow down to Gen 2 and further still thereafter.

Let me pause for a minute. Perhaps laying the problem out this way may have produced concern or anxiety about any information flowing downstream about what you might leave for your heirs. Maybe you feel that you should gather up your children and order them to keep things completely secret as wealth moves down to them — and to have them one day encourage their children to do the same. But with the way laws are trending, and the way information flows more generally within family systems, this isn't a long-term strategy for success. Putting your head in the sand is not only a recipe for failure, it may not even be an option.

Rather than double down on trying to prevent the information flow and all other aspects of inheritance, it's much healthier to realize that the success of a transfer of wealth into the third generation is more in the hands of your children and grandchildren than in your own. You might as well give your next gens the responsibility and tools they need to rise up to the challenge.

This can be really difficult – particularly for those that are used to running things, like most successful entrepreneurial wealth creators are. But if the difficult thing to do is also what will inevitably happen, not acknowledging the determinative role of the next gens requires a pretty high level of denial. And the longer it goes on, the greater buildup of "pressure" that will ultimately get released more quickly than can typically be processed well by those kept in the dark for decades. Sometimes when an inheritance gets spent or managed poorly, you'll hear people say that the patriarch and/or matriarchs must be "spinning in their grave." Perhaps. But keeping your future beneficiaries at arms-length regarding what's to come might be the equivalent of pre-ordering your casket with a spin cycle setting. Let's not do that.

Ok. I'm sure I've made my point. But I haven't necessarily given a picture of what I mean by giving over success. So let me summarize what I think that looks like:

- You recognize that you cannot mandate who your children or grandchildren are or will be.

- You recognize that you cannot "order" how your children or grandchildren will behave or think about wealth or otherwise.

- You recognize that your children and grandchildren have primary agency over who they are and who they will be.

- You recognize that your children have primary agency over how they raise their children, even as it relates to what you leave behind.

- Assuming they are old enough, you move from parent/ child dynamics to parent/adult child dynamics.

- You move from pronouncements and directives to conversations and collaboration with the adult next gens (and perhaps a bit earlier than that, too, as we'll discuss later).

Sound a bit overly broad to you? That's not necessarily unfair. At the same time, I see these as some of the "big rocks" that need to be included in almost any successful, healthy, positive generational wealth transfer.

WHAT IF WE DIDN'T LEAVE AN INHERITANCE TO OUR CHILDREN?

Perhaps you're considering another solution to the dangers of wealth transfers that we haven't really addressed yet: limiting or eliminating what passes down to the children at all. If inherited wealth has all these risks, why take the chance that an inheritance will ruin anyone in the family? It's a reasonable question. It can be a clarifying one, too. Wrestle with it. What do you think are the positives to leaving an inheritance? Do they outweigh the negatives/risks associated with leaving an inheritance? How might you answer questions like these differently as to each potential inheritor?

As these questions are asked and answered in a family, however, there needs to be a recognition that the family environment is not static. It can be re-directed and re-shaped – at least to an extent – to be more positive. But it takes work. Because humans tend to want to avoid this kind of hard work, there may be temptations to pull an inheritance off the board.

While that may solve some of the negative impacts of wealth, it doesn't do anything to foster a healthier dynamic and relationship with wealth in the family as a whole nor in individual family members. However you and your family answer the questions we're considering here, and whatever decisions you might make, I strongly encourage you to take on the parenting/grandparenting/stewardship work that would lead to stronger next gens.

As further encouragement not to avoid this hard work, recognize that not leaving (or significantly limiting) an inheritance also has its risks. Financial spiraling and poor decision-making can arise with or without the inherited dollars – and can be caused by disappointment or resentment that the inheritance didn't come or that "mom/dad didn't trust me" or whatever lens the non-inheritor might look through when the money doesn't arrive. Part of being a positive influence within your family is dealing with what the reality is within your family and within yourself. That doesn't mean you won't have a plan that is aggressively charitable in nature or that the inheritance to the next generations won't have some limits to them – but part of how to not ruin your kids with money is setting them up so that they wouldn't be ruined by a lack of money either.

9

Release the Definition
Of Success

We have one more thing to work through before getting more directly into the work: I suggest you need to release the definition of what success looks like for your legacy planning. Not a full release. Not a release that removes you from the process entirely. But a release that allows for significant input and involvement of your children, grandchildren and beyond in determining what success with wealth looks like in your family.

When it comes to this subject of passing on values or otherwise fostering a positive transfer of wealth across generations, the typical path involves a focused effort in determining what the senior generation's values are, what practices and priorities they want to pass along regarding wealth, and how they can accomplish their goals. That's all good stuff. I would not remove any of that from the process. But:

- If the children and grandchildren's values don't line up with those of the senior generation, they will pursue their own values.

- If the children and grandchildren do not agree with the senior generation's goals they won't work to advance them – and almost certainly would undermine their achievement.

- If the children and grandchildren's sensibilities on wealth are different, they are not likely to be abandoned in favor of those of the senior generation simply by being told that they are superior or important.

The next generation is made up of individuals with their own view of the world. And because they have the advantage of where they stand in time, they will eventually find themselves in the "first chair" when it comes to implementing and defining family values. But you ask, can't we address that in our estate planning? Let's explore that subject by considering a commonly discussed vehicle to encourage certain values[16] in next gens: the incentive trust.

The idea of an incentive trust is simple: the person creating the trust ties distributions to desired behaviors from the

---

16   It might be worth mentioning that I am assuming that the senior generation will identify positive values and goals. This is not an indictment of "old fashioned" or "outdated" values or goals coming from the senior generation. Far from it. In fact, most values and goals that members of the senior generation identify would likely be viewed as having a timeless, positive element to them when communicated properly. On the other side of the coin, though, I'm also not assuming that the junior generation(s) will have negative values or goals. So this isn't a conversation about better or worse. Rather, I am exploring how the senior generation needs, and in many ways is dependent on, the participation, involvement, and contribution of the next generations not only in the achievement of whatever the goals might be – but also in the determination of what the family's goals will be.

beneficiaries. These behaviors can include maintaining a high enough GPA, earning a college degree, earning a sufficient level of income, accomplishing certain training or mentoring – frankly, just about anything you can think of.[17] They can also tie access or distributions to more broad and subjective behaviors or beliefs, with a third party determining whether the favored behaviors or beliefs are sufficiently honored and adopted. On its face, there are some attractive qualities to this approach. After all, parents like to see their kids achieving things that they think of as admirable. And now there is a built-in financial incentive to achieve them.

Unfortunately, the carrot and stick approach of an incentive trust is only indirectly designed to develop good character. It only appears direct. While earning a sufficient level of income, as an example, might be the behavior sought, the manifestation of that behavior does not automatically mean that the beneficiary will prove themselves to have a good work ethic or be particularly industrious with their talents and abilities. They've just proved that they can earn a certain level of income to secure a particular distribution. And if it is an incentive trust that matches distributions to demonstrated earned income (a fairly typical structure for these types of trusts), it's not difficult to see how the incentive presented becomes an incentive to work half as hard as they otherwise might without the incentive.

---

17 A quick legal sidebar: most US states do not allow for conditions on inheritance that are tied to marriage, religious affiliation or actions, political affiliation or positions, or any number of highly personal actions or thoughts that sometimes are of very high importance to a trust's creator. While I'm not a fan of incentive trusts, I want to note that the law relevant to you and your situation may limit how far you can take the concept.

These structures also have a high risk of negatively impacting a beneficiary's self-sufficiency, sense of responsibility, or even their motivation to achieve to their capabilities. While incentives impact behaviors, the message that often comes across to beneficiaries is that they can't be trusted to make good choices on their own, that they're not sufficiently self-motivated, or they need someone to manage their behavior. Consequently, incentive trusts tend to have a minimizing effect (at least to adult beneficiaries) that may lead to extended or effective financial dependency and immaturity.

I acknowledge that I have painted a fairly negative view of incentive trusts. But without regard to their merits, the point is that we cannot confuse desired behavior with the achievement of long-lasting legacy goals or the manufacturing of virtuous character. So, if a primary goal would be for the subject beneficiary to develop into the kind of person that would naturally make positive choices regarding family, finances and personal growth, we should focus our efforts on achieving that. Not just on what we think that looks like. The experience of positive behaviors through incentives is a type of fool's gold that is easier to obtain, measure and draft documents for — but like fool's gold, the results will have little worth when considered against what you really want to see in your children and grandchildren.

Is there anything else that can do the job that an incentive trust just can't? I'm not sure there is. But I do know what the next most common discussion is on how to implement structure to try to foster character: the garden variety trust managed by a third-party trustee who is the sole determiner of what is disbursed, when it is disbursed, to whom it is disbursed and for what purposes it is disbursed. This is generally implemented with a directive – although often just an implicit one – that the trustee give due consideration to the values of the trust's creator in all these decisions.

This type of tried-and-true trust structure with a non-beneficiary trustee is a classic and necessary tool for any estate planning attorney to have in their toolkit. In these arrangements, the trustee can guide the beneficiaries with regard to budgeting, spending, investing, and basic life planning at an early stage when they might lack the character, competency, and capacity[18] to handle the funds well themselves. But can this process foster character, competency, and capacity? Or is it just a bridge to allow for those characteristics to have time to develop in the beneficiaries in question?

I think the answers to these questions are a bit of a mixed bag. On the one hand, as we've already explored, having too much wealth too early in the process can have a significant and detrimental impact on a beneficiary's character, competency, and/or capacity to manage wealth. The protective aspects of the trust may therefore be worthwhile and may be necessary for minor and young adult beneficiaries. On the other hand, while some beneficiaries do just fine with a little bit of "bump steering" along the way, other beneficiaries will not take advantage of the experience of working with even the highest quality trustee. For those beneficiaries, the structure can keep them from over-spending their inheritance, but will not necessarily

---

18 Check back to Chapter 4 for a reminder of why these three considerations are mentioned.

encourage progress towards becoming a full-fledged financial adult who incorporates the inherited funds into their financial experience well.

Sorry if I'm overdoing it again on trust structure. Designing and implementing trusts, and watching the design and implementation of trusts by others, has been a big part of my professional life. As important as design and implementation are, experience has shown time and time again that structure in and of itself cannot create or ensure specific results. Further, the persistency of "shirtsleeves to shirtsleeves in three generations" even with all kinds of trust structures having been implemented sure seems to indicate that there isn't a trust structure that overcomes human nature. At least not one that we've found yet.

Rather than put too much weight on trust structures then, we're back to the hard work of developing your family's definition of success and fostering an environment that is supportive of achieving that success. Let's talk about how to do that:

First, I strongly suggest that you have clarity on what you think success looks like. If you were able to wave that magic wand, what does success look like to you? But you object, "didn't you just say that it's not for me to define success?" Not exactly. I said to "release the definition." Not to discard any input you might have. Your input will be vitally important and that's why I noted my belief that the exercise of identifying the senior generation's goals is a positive and important exercise.

Second, once you've identified what success looks like to you, share it with the next generations as appropriate to their age and financial maturity. Then step back. Ask them what they think and let them say what they think. Not just what they think you want them to think. What would they honestly add or subtract from what you've shared? Where do you all line up? Where do you differ?

Third, be explicit about your shared goals and orient your planning and actions to their accomplishment. You and your children (and maybe grandchildren) will then have the ability to hold each other accountable in a positive way – because you now have shared goals that you all have a direct stake in.

The above can work out effectively and smoothly in families with high trust and strong cohesiveness. Of course, almost every family has differences and disconnects that can create friction. Also, those family systems with a higher concentration of "power" or "respect" in the senior generations may find that the next generations are less forthcoming about their differences and disconnects – and sometimes that dynamic is sufficiently weighty to prevent sharing even when a high level of trust exists. Regardless, if the senior generation genuinely invites the discussion and involvement of the younger generations, it almost always goes better.

In this process, there is an identification of what your family is all about – or at least what it aspires to be. In my family, I look at my four children and see such different people. Their personalities are so varied. Their personal interests, concerns, and approaches to life and its challenges are unique to each of them. But at the same time, they are also all Shillers. We can identify aspects of what makes us, "us." Some are harder to put into words and some just have to be experienced. But there still are things that go along with being members of the same family.

By understanding your commonalities, you elevate the collective family. By giving voice to individuals in their expression of what it means to be part of your family, you elevate each individual member while also realizing an enhanced sense of responsibility, accountability, and connectedness to the family overall. When both are done well, you can then get to the business of being your family with a part of that effort being the stewardship and application of your family's wealth.

As to your role in that, if you are in the senior generation position, I think it's helpful to think of the collective goal as your own. Otherwise, you'll be busying yourself trying to achieve the unachievable goal of replicating yourself in those who are not you. Something much more achievable, and more satisfying, would be focusing on the shared essence of your family, adding and expanding on what that essence is, and seeing others you love do the same to the benefit of the family as a whole and its future members.

As you get into the work of determining what makes your family your family – that essence – as contextualized to your wealth transfer planning, let me help you avoid some common missteps that come up frequently: confusing values and virtues. Maybe I can best illustrate this with a story.

A business owning family has experienced great financial success. The business has been around for a while, and the family is in the end stages of a positive transition of day-to-day leadership and primary stock ownership from Al, the founder, to Brittany, the founder's daughter. One of the other children, Carl, came into the business a few years ago and has been a great help to the internal operation of some aspects of the business. So far, so good.

Brittany, along with Al, continue to bat around ideas for how to grow the business and generally expand. Over time, several opportunities that seem almost too good to be true come to light. Each one an easy bolt-on to their existing business and Brittany and Al feel that each new thing will be a certain, big winner. Carl had never been part of those types of conversations in the past, but Brittany and Al decide that given his now three years of involvement that they should invite Carl to participate in the next opportunity. So they lay out the numbers, their excitement for the project, and best of all – Carl can get in with only putting up about $250,000 of cash – which they happen to know he has based on bonuses associated with his employment with the business, etc.

Carl is thankful that his sister and father have offered to bring him into the mix. He asks for some time to think about it. Although Al and Brittany don't know what there is to think about, they tell Carl to take all the time he needs. Several weeks pass and Al and Brittany are both confused. They tell Carl they have to move on this soon, and if they don't hear back within the week, they'll proceed without him because the window to act is closing. That week passes with no word from Carl, so Al and Brittany move ahead without him. Dumbfounded by Carl's silence.

The same scenario plays out more or less the same a few times more, leaving both Al and Brittany not just confused, but also frustrated. And disappointed. And, at least as to Al, a bit angry. How could Carl snub them multiple times when they're just trying to give him an easy win? Doesn't he value the family and the family's business? If nothing else, doesn't he want "free money?"

All this transpires, including the buildup of disappointment in Al and Brittany over Carl's intransigence, without understanding what's really going on: Carl just isn't entrepreneurial in the same way as Al and Brittany are. No matter how certain the outcome, he just doesn't have the same comfort level in putting $250,000 on the line that Al and Brittany do. And unsurprisingly Carl doesn't make the same decisions that his father and sister do.

Does that make Carl a bad person? Of course not. Not being entrepreneurial doesn't make one good or bad. Does Carl's risk aversion mean that he doesn't care about the family or the family's business? The answer again is of course not. It's a difference, not a flaw. By simply moving away from equating differences as defects, Al and Brittany can more clearly focus on all that Carl brings to the table. He's a hard worker. He's a winsome ambassador of the company both with employees and people in the community. He's a good son, and a good brother. He's a contributing member of the family and the family's business. And the next time one of the sure things comes up, Al and Brittany can move forward without Carl's participation and not think less of him for not wanting to join in.

I've seen the dynamics described above play out dozens and dozens of times, and I've heard similar stories many times from others, too. Sometimes, the issues blow up and it takes a fair amount of effort to recover from the fallout. Sometimes a simple realization that measuring something by their values (in the above example, entrepreneurialism) versus by their virtues (in the above, perhaps industriousness would be a good counterpoint) does the trick.

What about you and your situation? Are you imposing your values – which are subjective and neither positive nor negative – on your children or grandchildren? Or are you encouraging and lauding virtues – which are objective and universally positive? This seemingly small pivot on choosing what measuring stick to use can make it profoundly easier to release the definition of success to the next generation.

NEXT STEPS

The most concrete thing that is in this chapter is the identification of virtues and values of importance within your family. And I encourage you to spend some time thinking through which virtues and values are important to you. Inquire of your children and grandchildren what's most important to them – and also what stories you might be able to refer back to for your parents or grandparents on these matters. Head to www.markshiller.com/resources/ for more tools and resources on this subject.

What's not as concrete is the turning over of defining success and overriding goals and primary virtues and values. I submit that this is as much a change of posture and moving to an open hand, if you will, as opposed to a closed hand regarding your family's future. Sometimes this is easy – but way more often than not it is really difficult. Gather others around you to help you stay the course and learn to embrace the uncertainty as best you can.

Get After It

PART THREE

10

Engaging the Youngest Family Members

In this third part of the book, I'm going to try to be a bit more specific and practical with what you can do to "get after it" and provide actionable steps for you to take now. This presupposes that you now better understand the problems associated with generational wealth transfers and have co-developed your goals with the other stakeholders in your family's success. Or at least a decent start on the work regarding discerning and defining your family's shared goals and objectives. In many ways, it is work that unfolds over years and generations – so you shouldn't wait until you feel that task is "done" to move forward. It will be an ongoing conversation among your family's generations that will always be open.

Regardless, you're here. In this now. So you'll need to contextualize what you do based on the present circumstances within your family. Who's ready to participate in the conversation and who isn't? Who is solid on their feet when it comes to these matters and who isn't? How do the in-laws (or future in-laws) factor in? And so on as to a thousand other questions. While how to engage with these matters can sometimes present itself clearly in individual conversations, this book is a broader conversation trying to speak to individuals, couples, and families who are all at different points in time with different generational considerations. I'm going to first approach this last part of our discussion by giving consideration to the various "stages of life" of family members and common activities that families of wealth might pursue in each stage to steward wealth well generationally.

With that as a set-up, let's start with a few general thoughts about how to approach minor and younger adult family members. These are the children or grandchildren who haven't fully entered that maturation process that might often be viewed as beginning and ending within the ages of 25 to 35 or so. See Chapter 4 for a fuller discussion of these stages, but I'll just assume for the balance of this chapter that we're talking about how to deal with family members up until the point they leave the home, complete the bulk or all their education, and perhaps have a few years of experience out in the real world.[19]

At the earliest stages of life – let's say the first ten years or so – much of the learning regarding values and finances is observational. Osmosis is a powerful force early on. That's frankly one of the reasons I stress the importance of managing your own behavior to fully align with your goals – even before you think your children would have a sense of money matters. If you want your young children to be temperate in their spending when

---

19   If we were together, we could discuss what qualifies as being out in the "real world." It's beyond the scope of this book to define that – but I do note that there are significantly different ideas about what would qualify from one family to the next.

they're older, the best way to teach temperance to a 5-year-old is to practice temperance in your own spending. Same applies for your grandchildren. You will accomplish a lot if you walk the walk and are conscious of the direction you're headed.

I'm not sure there is a better strategy for fostering virtuous character in your youngest family members than practicing what you will (at least eventually) preach. If you have children in this stage of life, I encourage you to think deeply about this. A lot. And be honest with yourself, your spouse, and others, about where your actions might not quite match up with your stated values and course correct as necessary. This feels like an "unfun" thing as I type it. But it'll likely be the most important thing to do throughout your life to establish a solid foundation in your youngest family members. Before we move on, though, let me say one more thing about this point.

For families that are engaging in this process where the initial wealth creators are the senior generation, it is not unlikely that the creation of wealth, or at least the realization of the level of its creation, comes after the children are through their first ten years or so. In fact, it's likely that some or all of the children are out of the house when these issues come into focus. But that doesn't mean you should just skim past this as a non-relevant topic. Rather, this analysis will be relevant for the children to work through as to their own children (the wealth creator's grandchildren). The same will also apply for the other stages of life as this is not just about Gen 1 and Gen 2, but a subject across all future generations in a family.

I get questions all the time about how to engage kids who are old enough to have real conversations regarding finances, personal and familial responsibility, and so on. The topics vary from how much to share with your 10-year-old, your 15-year-old, your 20-year-old, etc. regarding your wealth, "allowance" amounts and systems, the level of a child's financial participation in college or other educational expenses, and the like. There are some wonderful resources out there that I could and do recommend.[20] And I will share a few of my thoughts with you. But let me first share with you a story about the limits of advice on these matters drawn from my own experience with my children on the topic of allowance.

My wife and I have been intentional about establishing rites of passage for our children. They have ranged from special trips with our children at certain ages, celebrations for various milestones reached, and so on. We wanted each of our children to have some intentional moments that would focus on him or her as they grew and matured. This also helped establish an orderly process for us to give more agency and autonomy to each child along the way.

With respect to money, we also wanted an incremental process towards greater independence for our children in their last years "in the nest." When their first year of high school began (roughly age 14 in the US) we allotted a set amount of money to be available each month to our children but paired it with an increased level of responsibility for certain expenses. Each succeeding year was coupled with a

---

20   Again, you can find resources related to this and others subjects of relevance in this book by going to www.markshiller.com/resources/.

reduction in the monthly amount and an increase in the child's financial responsibilities.

In this system, we had minimal "catches" for each child to get the next month's outlay. One was that our kids had to let us know what they did with the prior month's sum. They didn't have to justify their spending choices. They just had to tell us how they spent their allowance and other funds in that month. By doing so, we were communicating that we trusted our child to manage his or her money as long as they were paying attention.

For the most part, this system worked out as hoped with our oldest son. He was diligent with his "reporting" to us – and he learned that missing deadlines meant that he missed out on a month's allowance. There were a few instances where he had to go without on this or that because of where he was at in terms of his available cash. And as much as we might have wanted to in a couple of instances, we didn't bail him out – otherwise we felt that the learning would have been lost. Regardless, this experience seemed to allow him to learn how to prioritize spending needs, budget, and gain other basic financial skills and understandings to a satisfactory degree. All good things that served him well in college and beyond.

We applied the same approach to our second child who was three grades younger. And it was a completely different experience. As any parent of more than one child will attest - each child is unique. Different results shouldn't have been surprising, then, right? But given our second son's modest spending needs and slightly higher income from a job here or there, there would be many months where we didn't get a report and he didn't get the cash. And he had no problem with that. After all, he had what he needed and money left over.

So round two of this system had multiple months where the "cost" of a missed month (or two or three) to him was essentially zero. Which also meant that the corresponding lessons that we thought would come from the experiencing that cost didn't happen either.

Why tell a story of what could easily be viewed as a failed approach then? As I see it, although the structure did not work out as planned for all our children, the results suggest that our approach wasn't a failure. Even though the experience between our first two (and our third and our fourth, for that matter) was quite different, each child ended up with many (maybe all?) of the values and skills we hoped would be bolstered by the structure. In retrospect, I think the key was that putting this "system" in place opened conversations with our children, transferred responsibilities to them over time incrementally, and gave them the opportunity to make real, independent financial choices. Each child displayed growth in financial responsibility and maturity. So in that sense, the end results look more like success than failure.

The other reason I tell this story is to emphasize that there isn't a magic approach or formula that will lead to financially responsible adults every time. Although I cobbled together some of the best aspects of approaches taken by families who seemed to have had successful experiences on this subject with their children, and our results with our firstborn suggested that we had a great thing going, it was obvious early on in round two that we weren't working with a one-size-fits-all strategy. What we did have, and what we retained, was intentionality about what we were getting at and why. And each of our kids reacted to that intentionality, and in some ways met us in kind, with how they worked out their thoughts on financial matters, personal responsibility, the meaning they'd attach to material things, and so on.

Perhaps I'm getting into vagueness again. So let me give you some Do's and Don'ts in this minority and young adulthood stage:

- Do start giving smaller but increasing levels of responsibility and agency over money -- starting around age 10 – 13 and progressively more along the way thereafter.

- Do allow your children to take some missteps regarding finances and allow them the time and space to learn from them.

- Don't share everything regarding your finances while your children are in the process of maturing. The knowledge of what is held by the family can sometimes be as damaging to a not-yet-mature beneficiary as it would be if they actually had it in their hands.

- Do think through what level of cash (or credit) availability might be harmful for your children (or others in the family), and at least annually reconsider/recalibrate as needed as to what that level is.

- Do provide resources regarding financial literacy and competency. Your financial advisors can be a great help here – but make sure they have a clear sense of what boundaries and preferences you might have regarding these matters so that they can be in alignment with your family's objectives. Good advisors want to be helpful, but they won't necessarily have full knowledge of your preferences from their work with you.

In addition and extension to the above, the following items I submit are relevant at all stages of a beneficiary's life - and therefore will be repeated at the end of the next couple of chapters that follow for completeness.

- Don't use money as a weapon or a force to coerce certain behaviors out of your children or grandchildren.

- Don't tie money to love, affection, or the personal worth of your children. Same goes for sharing information regarding wealth as an attempt to curry favor/love/relationship/intimacy with your children.

- Do set expectations regarding the "shareability" of any information that you do choose to share regarding your family's wealth or income. As you decide what to share and what not to share, give some thought as to what you'd be OK having re-shared by your child with your child's friends and their families. Be especially cautious regarding what you do share at this stage!

There are three other subjects that I think are worth talking about before leaving our conversation on how to approach the youngest family members – post-secondary education, vocational development, and living independently. Recognizing that there are cultural aspects and norms concerning these matters, and acknowledging that opportunities can be very different from one location/country to the next, these transition experiences and the time in which they occur make them typically very important to the maturation process.

Let's talk about the education and vocational development and living independently topics together. I view them as a whole because of their common pitfalls and how similar concerns present themselves in one or the other of the two. Everyone has stories about how their first several years out of the house went poorly, multiple stories about others who didn't do well once they left the nest, or both. If you think about this for even just a moment, I'd bet that someone (maybe yourself) will come to mind pretty quickly. Perhaps the person you're thinking of recovered well. Perhaps they never did. But for those who did recover well, they almost to a person would prefer that their children not take a similar path.

This is not an academically rigorous treatment of the topic, as you've no doubt picked up on. It's also not a book that deals with the impact of mental health considerations and significant dysfunction in relationships that can impact how someone acts when outside the sightlines of their parents. Being honest about those considerations and addressing them responsibly will be critical to success. But if we put them to the side (just for our discussion here, of course), the secret sauce is making sure that each child has purpose, ownership, and accountability for this phase of life. Here are some quick thoughts on how to approach a few of the main factors in this stage of life:

Education

- In the college selection phase, even if you are going to cover the cost of education regardless of the amount, involve the child in the financial stewardship decision-making that goes along with the experience – especially if in a situation, like that in the United States, where post-secondary education expenses can vary wildly from institution to institution and can result in significant financial outlays.

- If you are covering 100% of the educational costs, be extra diligent in establishing what responsibility and accountability rests with the child regarding how they conduct themselves and pursue their studies.

- If you are covering only a portion of the costs, bring your child into the discussion about why you have come to the cost sharing arrangement you selected and how your child might cover their share. Note, this can be an approach that can tie to the college selection process as now your child is making an impactful, personal financial decision for themselves. They will have a voice in deciding whether, for example, paying for half of the more expensive school is worth it. Or as another example, if the child is responsible for everything over a certain dollar amount, do they want to take on that extra cost?

- Think about what happens if things go poorly. Is that determination a shared decision? Is it objectively determined by something like grade point average? Is there a "mulligan" or "do over" mechanic built into the system? Lay these matters out specifically and in advance as best you can. And, if something wasn't covered prior to the child heading off to school, address the matter as soon as the unconsidered issue arises.

Living Independently

- There are a million articles about how more and more children are returning to live with Mom and Dad for longer and longer periods of time in the US. These articles mostly reflect a changed experience in certain sub-cultures (even if the most predominant ones as of this writing) – so I want to acknowledge that the next few comments may not be pertinent (or at least not in the same way) in contexts where multi-generational living arrangements are more common and expected. With that caveat, in many US contexts "living in your parents' basement" is typically seen negatively. Perhaps as a result, there aren't common constructs that allow for continued personal development and maturity in those settings. Accordingly, you and your child might need to create expectations and norms and contextualize them to your family if he or she is going to live in your house for an extended period as a young adult.

- Your adult child needs to practice adult financial behavior and have adult financial responsibilities to complete their maturation process. Paying 100% of their living expenses has its consequences. So too does keeping them on your cell phone plan at age 30 even if you get a great discount.

- If your child is not progressing in financial maturity – whether living at your home or living on their own with you covering the costs – you have to be ready to make a change. Their maturity is more important than their, or your, comfort.

This chapter could easily be much longer and more in depth. But I hope this "breeze through" survey of the subject is of help. Now, let's move on to the Danger Zone.

NEXT STEPS

Now that we're in the "Get After It" section of the book, I'm going to give you a few challenges - recognizing that some of these "stage of life" sections might not all be presently applicable. Regardless, I hope they're helpful!

- Spend some reflection time evaluating how you're doing in modeling the financial values to younger family members.

- Decide what rites of passage and moves you should make in giving increased responsibility to the younger members of your family in ways that align with your family's primary values and goals. Be sure to involve other stakeholders, especially the subject individual's parent or parents.

- Lessons on character should be a focus from the earliest age. Emphasis on financial competency requires a different kind of skillset and type of comprehension. While that means such lessons might not be primary for the first five to ten years of life, work on financial competency should be folded in with continuing character building activities.

- Come up with a series of questions about wealth and money to ask your younger next gens and repeat them annually. Keep track of the answers and see how they evolve over time. If it's helpful, the kind of questions I'm thinking of might sound like: What should you do with the money you have? What responsibilities does someone with money have? What are things that you own? What does our family own together? Those are just a few examples to get you started – but make sure your questions are your questions.

- Listen for and to your children's perspective on matters of wealth and finances. When they share something notable and beneficial, let them know and act on it if it includes a challenge to do better. They will surprise you if you let them.

- Readers with the youngest beneficiaries might be tempted to skip the exercise of memorializing family values. If that's you, make it a priority instead!

11

Getting Through the "Danger Zone"

I t's time for us to discuss the "Danger Zone." Sounds ominous, doesn't it? Maybe a bit over-dramatic? Perhaps. But I am convinced that this particular stage of life is where someone's financial maturity, competency, and capacity are established – and most susceptible to outside influences. Shifts to the good or to the bad, so to speak, are much more likely to occur in young adulthood than in the latter half or latter two-thirds of life. Furthermore, the pressures and pulls on young adults who have available wealth to make less desirable/beneficial choices are quite strong – perhaps stronger than ever. And young adults face these pressures and pulls when they are either no longer under, or no longer taking advantage of, Mom and Dad's oversight. This stage of life is truly dangerous.

It is easily observable – and I do not think I need to spend time convincing you of this – that once someone reaches a certain point in their lives, the "cement sets" on many or most of their habits, philosophies, values, etc. on money and many other matters. To be sure, people can and do make changes in even the most core aspects of their personal beliefs and values throughout their lives. But things tend to be much more static later in life than earlier on. Mistakes[21] in this stage are harder to recover from and good results tend to be more persistent.

There is always a tension when discussing matters of financial expenditures to not project too much of one's own values onto another's choices. What one person or family decides is a baseline lifestyle and appropriate spending will vary significantly from one person or family to the next. Keep that in the front of your mind as you think through this subject – and know that I'm trying to speak generally despite the risk of my own biases seeping into the conversation.

But here's the thing: no one I know wants their children to be fully dependent on them financially if their children have the capability to provide for themselves. Even when they want their children to experience some of the benefits of the wealth they have, they don't want them to over-extend or to live too high of

---

21   "Mistakes" might be seen as a harsh word and one that carries a fair amount of judgment with it. I struggled a bit whether to use it here – and frankly words like this one throughout the book – because of that. Given the personal nature of the subject we're dealing with, calling less desirable choices or outcomes "mistakes" carries a risk that the individual who made the less desirable choices or experienced the less desirable outcome is seen as less desirable, valuable, worthy, etc., themselves. That should never be the messaging about any human being – especially messaging from a parent or grandparent to their child or grandchild.

That said, those less desirable choices and outcomes can have significant negative impact on a person's life experience. Using the harsher word is therefore intended to emphasize the importance and benefits of good choices and seeking good outcomes. We want those we love to experience more full and fulfilled lives. I therefore trust that taking this "risk" in word choice is worth it.

a lifestyle too soon. Yet here are a few common situations that come up anyway:

- Mom and/or Dad get the child an apartment that's more expensive than what the child's income could cover. Perhaps the rent is provided before the child has any income to contribute. This can impact financial and career decisions because the consequences of lost or lower income on accessible living arrangements are muted or unaffected.

- A similar situation might involve a significant gift/contribution to a home purchase for a child that is at a level beyond what the child's income could support. Or the child's ability to maintain the home is at risk when a major maintenance expense arises or if the child's income is lost or diminished for an extended period of time. In such an event, the child might not have sufficient personal resources to resolve the situation – and may therefore have nowhere else to turn but to the family and its wealth. If bailed out, the lessons associated with being over-extended could become lost to the child – especially if the situation repeats itself a second time. Or a third, or fourth, etc. And, if not bailed out, other issues arise.

- Parental support for investment opportunities identified by the child, but for which third party financing is unavailable or "under available" clouds the investment decisions of the child. That doesn't necessarily mean that the investment opportunities won't perform well or aren't desirable – but rather that potential, valuable lessons can be lost regarding what happens when you can't pull a deal together due to insufficient capital. Further, the provision of capital for no charge or at a "family discount" needs to be understood as distorting the economics of an investment decision and the conversations around pursuing them. Do those distortions lead to too easy entry into investment opportunities? Or too easy success on real estate or business investments?

- A classic issue arising in family businesses is when the family business owner gives his or her kids, grandkids, nieces, nephews, siblings, etc., jobs at the company that they're not ready for. These types of decisions are almost never made at the earliest stages of the first-generation wealth creator's efforts. They couldn't be. The money wasn't there yet. But once there is success and the ability to support additional individuals and families, whether through love or guilt or some other motivation, a founder might be tempted to offer a job to a family member too soon or promote someone into a job that's over their skillset and capabilities. These types of decisions usually crop up for family members in the Danger Zone – which means it could foreclose the young adult child/grandchild from developing into a more marketable and capable employee should the business be sold or otherwise suffer to the point that continued employment is unsustainable.

- Another, subtle issue that can crop up is the young heir/heiress treatment from others that could lead to an inflated sense of importance or accomplishment. Community recognition, involvement in soctietal or political causes at a higher level because of lineage as opposed to talents, flattery from family advisors or club staff, and similar experiences do not really advance someone's personal and professional development – but they might feel like it to someone who has not had outside experiences completely disconnected from their family's wealth and stature.

NOTE TO NEXT GENS

I don't hear it a ton, but multiple times I've heard adult children or grandchildren (usually grandchildren) lament that they are the ones that are supposed to "lose it all." They've heard the Three Generations Rule and heard it as a prophecy of their upcoming and inevitable failure or an unassailable attack on their character or capabilities.

Going through this conversation about the Danger Zone may bring these concerns and criticisms back up to the surface for you. If so, let me just remind you that the whole point of this book is that the fates of you and your descendants aren't set. Even if your parents and grandparents make every misstep possible, you can overcome them all and are the prime determiner of your success. Put the negativity to the side and pursue the best outcome for you and your family.

Let me give you one more point of encouragement. Those families that do well in transitioning to Gen 3 are far more likely to do well with transitions to Gen 4 and Gen 5. Perhaps that means that the hardest transition is from Gen 2 to Gen 3 – but it also means that you might be best positioned to create successful outcomes for multiple future generations. Personally, I would find that exciting.

There is another side of the coin to all of these and other like situations – a child's actual skills and talents can get dismissed by outsiders because they assume that any of the child's successes are only due to being born with a silver spoon in their mouth. Perhaps worse, the child will also likely have trouble figuring out what he or she was personally able to accomplish and what portion of those accomplishments were due to having a boost that others wouldn't have available to them. The inability to unwind these questions can lead to personal insecurity, diminishment of the capacity for wealth stewardship, and other significant problems. These are very consequential matters when present – and shouldn't be viewed as "balancers" against the countervailing concerns like those listed above.

Let me guess as to your thoughts right now: "I know all that." Or at least most of the above. Most people do. But if we know these things, why are these issues for next gens so persistent? Why do we keep seeing these same problems over and over again? Let's explore that a bit with a typical cycle with respect to a young adult in the Danger Zone when wealth is present:

1. Parent wants to give child a financial boost or feels guilty unless they do.

2. Child does not say no.

3. No hard boundaries/expectations are established regarding future help.

4. Lather. Rinse. Repeat.

5. Child's personal, financial strength and capacity is less likely to fully form.

The above patterns show up in loving, connected families as much as in families that have systemic challenges. An unhealthy family dynamic in these matters will involve some form of manipulation or weaponization of wealth by either or both the giver and receiver. This can be complicated, accelerated and exacerbated by divorce and other brokenness within a family system. While the results and consequences might be worsened, the general pattern is the same.

How then does the cycle get broken? There are three links to the chain where this could occur: (1) Mom or Dad could stop boosting; (2) the child could refuse future boosts; or (3) appropriate boundaries and expectations could be set and adhered to by all parties. Let's consider all three.

Parent(s) Stop Boosting

As the ones who "write the check," the parents always have the ability to not write the check. And if they don't, the chain is necessarily broken. Does this solve the problem? Well, maybe. Depending on how far down the road the boosting has gone, it may leave the child financially exposed and facing long-term, negative consequences. Frankly, it's usually the concern regarding these harms that keeps the parent from opting out of further contributions to the cycle.

When a parent unilaterally decides to stop boosting, it usually is uncomfortable and sometimes gets ugly. The parent has decided that the continuation of the cycle will lead to worse and worse consequences. And while they're probably right, cutting things off all at once is jarring to the child (as well as the family system) – and often occurs without the child being fully prepared for the ensuing consequences. I will cast more light on that in just a moment.

Child Refuses Future Boosting

A child refusing boosting is more common than you might think. Children may appreciate the things and comfort and opportunities that come with the boosts, but they also value the self-esteem and personal independence that comes with standing on their own two feet. In the middle is a tension that is difficult for a young adult to navigate through as they move from a position of full dependence in minority to full or close to full independence in adulthood. No small part of this difficulty is attributable to the fact that there generally is not a fixed point in time where a child is "cut off" in many families of wealth.

Unfortunately, a child's refusal isn't always long-lasting. If prior boosting has led to a greater personal asset base – particularly with real estate holdings that require tending and spending – then financial missteps and reversals might put the child in a position where they need to ask for a lifeline. Mom and Dad generally are the only ones to go to because the lending market won't take the risk (at least not without their participation). And who wants to see their child have a significant blemish on their financial history? And doing the repairs to the house will at least preserve its value, right?

Setting Boundaries and Expectations

Anecdotally, it seems to me that the boundary setting aspect is usually least focused on regarding breaking out of the cycle. It makes sense that this would be the case because it is the one part of the cycle that requires participation on both sides of the boosts. It also requires the most work and collaboration and alignment. And an evolution in the parent-child relationship. And usually hard choices. Ugh. Who likes those?

When dealing with hard-to-break behaviors and patterns, there are generally two paths: (1) immediate, "cold turkey" removal of the temptation; or (2) tapering removal. Which is appropriate depends on the nature of the behavior or pattern and how reliant or dependent the subject might have become. When it comes to money and financial support, usually tapering is the best choice – provided that the parties involved can come to mutual agreement about the process, the end point, the end goals, and the timing of the various steps to be taken.[22]

My guess is that for families of significant wealth, the first family member to get a copy of this book will be in the parent or grandparent position in the cycle. If there's sufficient interest, I may focus on the grandparent/grandchild dynamics in greater depth – but the point is, the first readers within the family likely have children or grandchildren who are somewhere in the cycle described above. Getting out of the cycle generally will require some nuance assuming that tapering is the right approach. While we could spend some time on that, tapering will be much more variable and dependent on the specific facts and circumstances. Let me suggest some Do's and Don'ts for a

---

22 Getting some guidance on this topic from skilled professionals or trusted friends can be very helpful here. Even better, though, is the establishment of these principles for the family as a whole in advance of a boosting cycle beginning for future entrants into the Danger Zone.

longer-term family set of expectations on the other side of the cycle or in advance of its beginning. I suspect that these may provide some guidance for establishing an end point goal and for providing some guideposts for establishing a tapering approach.

- Do talk about and get to agreement on the importance of financial independence and what that looks like in your family.

- Do agree on how much boosting is available, for what purposes, and at what stages/ages. To give an example, if a parent would like to provide a boost to get a first home, what is the dollar or percentage limitation on that boost? What responsibilities should the child consider as theirs before accepting the boost? What other conditions are there to receiving that boost? What impact does the local real estate market have? In other words, set boosting and/or lending "underwriting" standards for this type of transaction.

- Do discuss what happens if a boost recipient gets in over their head. Is there a one-time reprieve? Should the recipient be required to sell the asset if it cannot be independently maintained?

- Do share this conversation with your advisors and bring in appropriate advisors into the development of the principles and boundaries established.

- Do take advantage of therapists who can assist with any disconnects, dysfunctional relationships, and communication barriers/gaps. There's no shame in asking for needed/beneficial help.

And again, here are some of our "lifelong" Do's and Don'ts that not only apply to the boosting cycle, but all aspects of wealth conversations and interactions with your family members working their way through the Danger Zone:

- Don't use money as a weapon or a force to coerce certain behaviors out of your children.

- Don't tie money to love, affection, or the personal worth of your children. Same goes for sharing information regarding wealth as an attempt to curry favor/love/relationship/intimacy with your children.

- Do set expectations regarding the "shareability" of any information that you do choose to share regarding your family's wealth or income.

Before we move on from the Danger Zone, let's talk about what almost everyone wants to talk about in the Danger Zone – what do we tell "the kids" about our wealth and when? Of course, there's plenty of factors to consider: Are there younger siblings/cousins who might be affected by what is shared? What do they know already? How much wealth is there? How much wealth has been shared already? In other words, there are plenty of reasons to say, "it depends." Keep that in mind, but let me try to speak directly in a base case situation to the "how much to share and when" topic:

- Be more conservative with what you share the greater the wealth you have stewardship over.

- Do not share everything with a person upon their entrance into the Danger Zone.

- If a person is solidly on their way out of the Danger Zone, it'll be helpful to share everything (or at least most of it) with that family member.

- If a person is not in a place of personal, financial maturity, evaluate whether there is still work that can be done – but otherwise, you probably want to hold back on sharing information and communicate that you are doing so and the reasons why.

- If you can share things with a group of children/siblings all at the same time, that often has benefits for communicating common values across a family group within a generation. The spread of ages between oldest to youngest, or blended family dynamics, might, however, make this difficult or impractical.

- I usually suggest that full disclosure to next gens not occur prior to age 25 – and usually find that the comfort level and appropriate time frame for most families is later than that.

Always leave room for growth for family members who might be struggling to reach a desired point of maturity, character, competence and capacity – but you should also be clear on how to approach financial matters with someone who limps out of the Danger Zone with bruises and scars.

Let's move on to the next phase – after the cement sets and you've got what you've got.

NEXT STEPS

For those with beneficiaries in the "Maturation" stage, here are some potential follow ups:

- Consider what subjects have not had full communication - whether regarding education, financial support, etc. - and have any necessary conversation.

- If you're in a boost/dependency cycle, address it with the beneficiaries and any appropriate therapists or other advisors.

- If you can see a "boost" circumstance developing in the future, develop appropriate ground rules or parameters to lay out well in advance of writing the first check.

- Be intentional in seeking out the perspective of the young adult beneficiaries in your life. Take a posture of listening, but be ready to provide mentoring when the door is opened for that.

- I don't see this in every family, but this seems like the stage where sibling rivalries and disconnects can get calcified. You may need some professional guidance, but be thoughtful on the trajectory of relationships within a generation passing through the Danger Zone.

- Reflect on the level of confidence you have in these beneficiaries. If it's low for one or more, decide what to do about it - again with appropriate help and guidance.

12

When You've Got
What You've Got

Perhaps the title for this chapter/description of this next stage of financial and personal maturity sounds a bit defeatist and negative. I hope it doesn't come across that way – but I get why it might. While I strongly believe and affirm that humans can and do grow, learn, and mature over their entire lifetimes – including on core values and perspectives – as I've alluded to already, things do tend to change less on bigger things later in life. Maybe all the more so with respect to financial matters after young adulthood.

This subject comes up all the time in estate planning discussions when considering the structure of an inheritance for a beneficiary and when he or she would receive ownership or control over his or her inheritance. The most common age, when age is used as a metric, that parents seem to land on is typically somewhere between ages 25 and 40. While there may be uncertainty at what level of financial character, competence and capacity a beneficiary will be at that chosen point in time, there generally is a thought that eventually "you've got what you've got." And holding back the inheritance for another five or ten or twenty years isn't likely to produce any different results. If that's so, then we're done with this chapter, right?

Let's acknowledge that at this point we've got full adults who should have full agency over who they are. At this stage, more than ever, it's important to be clear that you do not have the power to force any change on another adult. Maybe you can sway behavior a bit through "carrots and sticks." But any meaningful, positive change that occurs regarding financial character, competency or capacity is not going to be effectuated by clever manipulation. And it certainly isn't going to appear by repeating high and lofty sounding principles over and over.

Putting aside their agency over who they are, you almost certainly have a much-reduced influence over next gens in this last stage just based on the lessened time you are physically present with them. Their lives are most likely busier with their or their kids' activities. Time with a spouse takes priority over time with a parent – as it should. Perhaps they have moved away and the distance and residency in another part of the country or world feels like it reduces your shared commonalities. You just don't have the same opportunities to affect change at this stage even if you wanted to. Since we don't have the time or access we need to effectuate change, we're done with this chapter, right?

Well, I haven't stopped writing yet. I must have something I want to share. And here it is: when they're adults, you need to stop trying to force your children or grandchildren to change. It's the wrong perspective and the wrong mindset. We covered this in some depth at the end of the previous section of the book – but it's easy to look at the arc of time in a child's life and forget at some point you're no longer "in charge."

NOTE TO NEXT GENS

This chapter could be tough to read if one or both of the following are true for you: (1) you're not where you want to be in terms of overall financial maturity (measured by overall character, competency and capacity) and/or (2) the senior generation underestimates your overall financial maturity. If the former, this chapter makes it sound like personal change is not very likely. While it is less common, how likely it is for you depends on you and your choices. Even though personal development may stall later in life for the majority, there are many, many grand stories of success forged later in life.

More likely for those Next Gens having difficulty with this chapter, though, is the latter. If you're in a good spot in terms of financial maturity (be very self-reflective about this topic, though) but aren't recognized for it, you're going to have challenges with your ancestors. That said, if you are seeking approval from someone in the senior generation who is withholding it, you and your family might be served better by focusing more of your attention on building up the generation to come. You will foster greater success by taking ownership of this and like challenges before you.

In Chapter 8, I suggested that you should give over the success of Gen 3 to the members of Gen 2. What I didn't say is that there's an element of letting go that's healthy even when Gen 2 isn't fully past the Danger Zone.[23] What you can and

---

23 The presence of significant dysfunctions, limitations, or harmful behaviors does, of course, impact all of what we're discussing. Here not "fully past the Danger Zone" means we simply have a gap between what is hoped for for a young adult family member and what has been achieved.

should do is acknowledge the impact of Gen 2 on Gen 3 and communicate that the success for the next generation (their children's success) is in their hands. Place as much confidence (or even more) in them as you can. Doing so establishes and communicates the challenge and gives the next generation awareness of the opportunity that is in front of them to benefit their children that they love and cherish. Being given this responsibility (which in many ways is just an acknowledgement of what is naturally the case) can be emboldening and affirming to Gen 2 and make them more likely to rise up to what the task requires.

I have seen many families stumble when Gen 1 tries to retain too much responsibility for the development of Gen 3 instead of relying on Gen 2's influence and position. Maybe holding on too long is exacerbated by extended lifespans and later-in-life inheritances. There's simply more time to try to do it yourself and your way. But the further outside of the Danger Zone someone gets, the lower the ability for an older generation to positively influence the younger. In some ways, the greater "statistical play" is increasingly becoming to focus on Gen 4. While that might be the right thing to do strategically or statistically, making that kind of a decision will also feel (to all involved) as giving up on a lot of potential success in Gens 2 and 3.

How about some Do's and Don'ts for this stage given the above?

- Do explicitly transfer ownership of nurturing the following generation's success to your children and establish that pattern for future generations within the family.

- Do acknowledge and admit your mistakes and missteps and view them as learning opportunities for how to handle things for the next generation. Note that there will be temptation to get defensive about how your children respond to these admissions. Try to resist giving in to it.

- Do give your children more rope on the subjects that come up than you might feel comfortable with at first. There likely will be some testing as to how serious you are about not taking control of the process from them. Stay strong and trust that they'll get it right. Or at least more right than what would otherwise be the case if you over-involved yourself.

- Don't wallow in any perceived "failure" or "defect" in your shepherding the prior generation to a stronger position. You are where you are. Do the best you can with where things stand and move forward.

- Do share your conversations and decisions with your advisors and bring your advisors into the process as appropriate without abdicating your involvement or removing your presence from the family's work.

- Do take advantage of therapists who can assist with any disconnects, dysfunctional relationships, and communication barriers/gaps.

And again:

- Don't use money as a weapon or a force to coerce certain behaviors out of your children.

- Don't tie money to love, affection, or the personal worth of your children. Same goes for sharing information regarding wealth as an attempt to curry favor/love/relationship/intimacy with your children.

- Do set expectations regarding the "shareability" of any information that you do choose to share regarding your family's wealth or income.

If addressing these issues head on is new for your family – which is probably the case for most readers – you will face some unique challenges. One is keeping those, including yourself, who need to be engaged in the process engaged in the process. This is especially important given the tendency to outsource hard things to others as a way to avoid them. I've seen this play out in a number of ways: (1) putting a trust together and signing it might feel like you've solved your wealth transfer concerns; (2) having a great financial/investment team might a feel strong enough support to carry any weight that your children or grandchildren cannot; (3) having an experienced trustee or other fiduciary in place after you're gone might feel like they'll take care of whatever comes up later; and so on. As positive and necessary as all those and similar approaches can be, you can't expect too much of your advisors or the structures they create. The best advisors won't let you fall into overreliance on them – at least not when they can see that it's happening. But that's not as easy as it might sound. Especially with advisors who so want to be helpful and caring. To minimize these issues, hold on (as a family) to the primary responsibility for your successes and be conscious of anything that might undermine that primacy.

Another tension/temptation that senior generation members will feel is to bypass the next generation's leadership as to the following generation. We've addressed this in the above discussion, but I bring it up again to highlight how this lands on that next generation. On their side, next generation members often feel uneasy that the rug is going to be pulled out from under them with respect to their leadership concerning raising and developing their children. This is particularly so when the senior generation is used to calling the shots (in business and in life). Contributions from the senior generation can easily be seen by Next Gens as intrusive or undermining of their authority, and even as an attempt to replace their authority. And that seems to be so regardless of how helpful or well-intentioned the senior generation's contributions might be. Building trust isn't easy – and it also has to be a team sport, with each side of the relationship playing its part. But recognizing what you are all facing and being open and transparent about the matter with each other will not hurt the process if everyone is acting in good faith and out of love for one another.

With all these caveats/warnings/concerns, what might you expect all this to look like and accomplish in your family? The biggest benefit is the opportunity for the next generation to step up not only for the benefit of the following generation, but for the experience that will also allow them to shape and mold themselves into stronger and more capable financial adults. Of course, they have to lean into the challenge – but in some ways the best way to learn is to teach. And who better to teach than a teacher who is fully invested in their students' successes?

Unfortunately, I haven't seen many families with Gen 2's that are a bit "behind schedule" implementing this type of approach. Some of this assuredly has to do with how little direct communication on these subjects has occurred in past generational wealth transfers – and how little of that has occurred in the current environment for wealth transfer. Another issue might be the mechanics of how challenges like these get raised generally. Consider the following family scenario:

> David and Talisha are in their 60's and are about 10 years out from their first significant foray into wealth and estate planning for their family. They've done well, and so has the plan – in the sense that the children now have sizeable trusts for their benefit. The problem is, at least as David and Talisha see it, their children have not yet gotten to where they want them to be. Maybe they don't see the kids as having as much "drive" as they had or feel like they spend too freely or some similar concern. Whatever it is, they're worried about how all of this might go over in the next 10 or so years – and how it'll eventually play out for their grandchildren.

> When they have their next conversation with a trusted advisor, this subject comes up and it moves from an update on how things are going to an emotional, animated discussion. The further the conversation goes, the more David and Talisha's concerns are bubbling up to the surface – maybe for the first time, or at least the first time spoken - and the trusted advisor wants to assuage their anxieties.

> What tools are available to the advisory team to respond then? Traditional responses might include locking down the access, input or control of the children and future generations to put up a firewall between them and whatever "too

much" access, input, or control is deemed to be. Another common response would be slowing down the next phase of planning that would put more funds downstream. Perhaps there would be a reduction of cashflow suggested. But what isn't normally suggested is having the "shaky next generation" chart the course to success or to call a meeting to collaborate on developing a shared response. That's not only the more difficult path, but it also takes longer and the results are less certain given the additional voices that would be brought in – and most good advisors want to have more immediate, definite solutions. So the tougher road is usually not taken.

No doubt the level of fear that accompanies giving up control to someone you're not sure is ready for the challenge presented is a huge factor in how families pursue multi-generational success with wealth. Some are much better at giving up control – although those who are also tend to have applied that approach in other areas of their lives and within their family. They tend to be further ahead on this skill than those who are used to achieving success through retention of control – and many wealth building success stories are traceable to retained control by talented and effective entrepreneurs and business owners.

If you're going to take or at least consider this more open-handed approach, it might be helpful for you to have a self-assessment of your readiness for the process of turning over control regarding the raising of the grandchildren and successive generations. And to seek help to manage the process, even if you're otherwise in a good position of readiness. Perhaps some quick self-assessment questions would be helpful:

Will Control Issues Get in the Way?

As they say, if you know, you know. But maybe you're not sure. Consider how many of the following statements might be true of you:

- You tend to be more focused on what you think needs to be accomplished than what others are saying in important conversations.

- You tend to give advice or criticism as much or more often when unprompted than when asked.

- You are not comfortable with being told you're wrong. Even when you are.

- You have a quick temper.

- You are uncomfortable with uncertainty.

- You are rarely not the leader in the room - whether in family or business settings.

If you answered in the affirmative for more than a couple of these, you probably should seek some assistance in working through the process of ceding control to the next generation. If you did not, recognize you could have a blind spot on this matter and might benefit from someone else working through these topics with you. Frankly, most people with controlling tendencies do not fully see themselves clearly on these matters. Regardless how you responded to the statements above, I would still encourage you to also discuss them with someone close enough to you that can not only provide good insight on how they apply to you but also would feel free enough to tell you what you might not want to hear. If you don't have anyone like that in your life, involve a professional to help you see the matter clearly.

Before going to print, I was challenged to consider the prevalence and impact of narcissistic personality disorders on wealth transfer experiences. Implicit in the discussion was the notion that there is a correlation between the drive to create wealth and the presence of narcissistic tendencies and issues in the wealth creators. And while that may be so, it's also clear that not all wealth creators are narcissistic. When they are, though, successful wealth transitions are exceedingly difficult because narcissists tend not to see or deal with the challenges they create for others. My encouragement for wealth creators with these issues, and for their spouses, children, and other descendants, is to seek appropriate, professional support and guidance in overcoming them. There may be more work to do, but these challenges can be met and results can be good.

Will the Younger Generation Get a Chance to Step Up?

You need to understand the history that your family has had in the past when making a pivot to ceding control. In a good percentage of families – particularly those with an entrepreneurial senior generation that were the primary wealth generators – a senior generation member has been positioned as the primary source for financial and wealth matters. In such cases, there is a strong danger that a vacuum will be created upon the loss of that senior generation member that can't effectively be filled quickly enough by other family members. This creates a risk that Gen 2 family members will not be seen as primary sources on matters of wealth when Gen 1 is no longer on the scene. This may have implications external to the family, but will also reduce a sense of stability for younger generations. Consequently, elevating the role of Gen 2 usually requires intentionality and a pro-active, long-term commitment to doing so by the senior generation. Which can be difficult because the fruit of that effort might not be seen for decades.

Will the Estate and Financial Plan Match the Approach?

Although I have made the case that the role of the people involved in an estate plan will have greater impact than even the best drafted document, a misalignment in the planning structure can cause problems in the event of an early death or incapacity of the senior generation. For example, say that a family begins a move to elevate the responsibility of the Gen 2 members with respect to Gen 3 mentorship and development. If the passing of a Gen 1 member leads to a shift in control over the bulk of the inheritance structure that is not supportive of this mentoring approach, it is quite easy for the transition to get a bit off the rails. For instance, direct funding of trusts for Gen 3 at the death of Gen 1 that leads to distributions to Gen 3 members (whether through document requirements or the exercise of trustee discretion) at too high a level could undermine Gen 2's mentorship or authority or positioning as to their children on financial matters.

As another example, perhaps the family is moving towards shared management and mentoring but the estate plan provides for a centralization of management and control after the death of Gen 1. While these and a host of other scenarios can potentially be overcome, it will be important to keep family structures as aligned and supportive as they can be of the family's long-term success strategies.

So now are we done with this chapter? Essentially, yes. The last point I'll make, though, is that sometimes you have to make hard decisions that limit access and control and authority for family members that are unlikely to handle a certain level of inheritance well. You should be slow to make those decisions, but when they're the right decisions, they're the right decisions. I encourage you to be as creative and thoughtful as you can be when holding things back from a particular beneficiary to allow them as much agency, independence, and responsibility as you can. Whatever approach is chosen should be as supportive of that beneficiary's potential as possible under the circumstances. But there are times when limits are appropriate.

NEXT STEPS

For those with beneficiaries that are past the Maturation stage, here are some potential follow ups:

- Consider what financial information you have kept close to the vest that should be shared with the next generation(s) and strategize how best to have needed conversations.

- Any conversation should be tied to the primary goals and values/virtues that are important to you and your family. Perhaps this is the subject you need to start with before sharing the balance sheet with your Next Gens.

- Reflect on how you might be keeping wealth or information on your wealth from next generation(s) members and what that says about them and also your view of them. If you have low confidence in one or more family members, decide what to do about it - again with appropriate help and guidance.

- Look for opportunities to release the responsibility for your family's success to the next generation - and then do so!

WHAT IF WE DON'T HAVE CHILDREN/GRANDCHILDREN?

We've spent a lot of time talking about the next generations. And it's certainly not unfair to say that a lot of the discussion has had an underlying assumption that the children will have children who have children who have children. That might be overly traditional - but it's also true that each reader at some point was the product of a child who was a child of another who was a child of another. So it's not necessarily the worst assumption!

Even so, we have to recognize that, particularly in more developed economies across the globe, many are choosing to have fewer children than in prior generations and more are choosing not to have children at all than would have done so in the past. Depending on where you're at in your life, maybe you don't have any certainty about whether you'll have children, grandchildren, great-grandchildren - or whether the family line might end in some far-off century. So what are you to do?

The first thing I'd point out is that uncertainty does tend to freeze people from taking action. If there are too many options to consider, many might just push things off and see how life plays out. There's a point to taking that approach - but also a significant danger that you never leave that place of indecision.

Perhaps there is a sadness or even a dread that goes along with thinking that you might not have further descendants. That's not how everyone might feel - but some certainly would. And as we've considered in many other contexts, when there is a difficult or unpleasant topic in front of us, it sure feels nice to just ignore it at least for a little while longer.

There might be any other number of considerations that come up for you. Perhaps the circumstances will change, but when do you plan as if they won't? Of course, I'll encourage you to do so now, but I'll also observe that people are much more likely to be comfortable addressing these kinds of questions when they're in their late 50's or early 60's with no kids or about 10 or so years later than that if their kids don't have kids.

I still would encourage earlier planning, but once you do start, you'll need to think through:

- Who will control the disposition of your assets if you do not have further descendants?

- What is the legacy you want to leave behind? Does that include friends or other family members? Your community? Charitable organizations?

- Who decides what to do if the family line ends long after you have passed?

- What input do collateral family members get with respect to your estate planning?

13

Getting the Most Out of Your Advisors

You made it! You've spent the time considering where your family is, you've worked together on establishing and communicating your family's values, philosophies, objectives, etc., and positioned the next generation to carry on your family's important work to see wealth transfer well across generations. But as important as it is that your family has the primary responsibility and activity for that success, you know that you don't (and can't) do it alone. So who needs to come alongside you to make sure things work smoothly and efficiently as well as in alignment with the course your family has charted?

Let's talk about the kind of advisors that families of wealth typically require. Of course, there will be a variance in what any individual person, couple or family might require – so there may be some categories of advisors that aren't needed in your particular circumstances. What's below, though, will be a fairly complete list of categories for most families that would be categorized as High Net Worth or Ultra High Net Worth. At levels of wealth in excess of the first tier Ultra High Net Worth category, there may be a place for additional types of advisors or greater emphasis on specialization within the categories. Likewise, at levels of wealth below what would be considered High Net Worth, you'll likely find a reduced need or advisability of certain categories of advisors. Also, please keep in mind that this is a general discussion that, like many others in this book, will require contextualization to your situation.

Qualitative Factors for All Advisors

Before talking about specific disciplines, let's start with a discussion of the kind of people you want on your team. There's not enough space to give a full treatment on this topic – but, for what it's worth, here are some qualities that I suggest you look for when selecting any advisor for you and your family:

1. The advisor should have regular experience working with people of your general net worth level.

2. The advisor should be good at their job and enjoy what they do. Don't discount the latter, as the two often go together. Rarely does someone who doesn't enjoy their vocation have the energy or take the initiative to get much better at what they do.

3. Your advisors should be regular communicators as appropriate to their discipline. Although you can set a different cadence, they should make themselves regularly available to you so that your conversations are as

likely to occur when things are flying high as they are when things are crashing and burning.

4. Your advisors should match you personally. While their temperament or personalities might be different from yours, they should at least have common values and the ability to align their work with your expressed values and personal sensibilities.

5. Your advisors should care more about you and your family as people than they care about "the account."

Investment Advisors

If you have a reasonable level of liquid assets, you will likely benefit from having an investment advisor. There are quite a few of them out there, though - over 280,000 investment advisors in the US alone.[24] Some work in one person shops while others work in firms with thousands of advisors. Some have very modest assets under management while others manage trillions of dollars for others. Credentials and processes and financial products offered can be all over the map, too. How can anyone choose from so many options?

Beyond the factors listed in the preceding section, I'd suggest that when selecting an investment advisor that you think not only about what your current investable asset level is – but also what it will be in the future. For instance, families with closely-held businesses or rental real estate portfolios often have relatively small amounts "in the market" while they are active in their business/real estate portfolio – but may eventually experience one or more liquidity events

---

24   US Bureau of Labor Statistics, May, 2022.

that will lead to a higher investable asset portfolio. In those cases, you'll want an advisor who can "keep up" with those expected/likely changes.

One other thought - and you could apply this to other advisors, too: when choosing an investment advisor for a multi-generational situation and set of goals, you should generally be seeking a long-term relationship. I rarely see people of wealth chasing that extra 0.1% of returns in any given year. Rather, they tend to be quite content working with quality people, giving quality service, with quality returns, over the long haul. If you get that, you'll be just fine.

Accountant/Tax Advisor

Proactive, thoughtful CPAs and other tax advisors – both for personal taxes and for business interests and property holdings – can add a lot of value beyond just getting your tax returns prepared and filed. Some accountants can naturally flow into proactive planning, while other quality CPAs might need a little push to do so. For higher net worth situations, you probably should place greater value on proactivity – but familiarity and fluency with the kind of structures and strategies that might need to be created or considered is highly important as well.

Estate Planning Attorney

If you have enough wealth to put your heirs at risk, you certainly should have a quality estate planning attorney as part of your team. This is my discipline and background, so I no doubt have some biases as to what that attorney should do and provide. Of course, you will want them to have the requisite technical expertise to know, recognize, and implement the techniques and strategies that your situation might require/suggest. But you also likely want them to be proactive and creative. Given the opportunity, as with the other disciplines, those attributes can be quite valuable. But it's also generally harder to get that out of estate planning attorneys than some of the other professionals on your team.

One reason for that difficulty is that estate planning attorneys are not generally in a position to have specific, regular interaction with their clients. Financial advisors need to make or consider adjustments many times throughout the year and connect with clients about the need to make (or not make) a move. Similarly, CPAs will have an annual connect point of a tax return that opens the door for fuller discussion. That's usually not the case with estate planning attorneys.

Additionally, lawyer-client relationships generally tend to be more reactive than they are proactive. I'm speaking generally, but lawyers tend to be very responsive when a problem arises but rarely are compensated or in a position to recommend strategies to avoid problems when they have not been asked to do so. That probably was exacerbated in the US given the always increasing estate tax exemptions ever since the 1997 tax act – an experience that is scheduled to come to an end in 2026. Simply put, the transfer tax planning environment in the US has gotten progressively better since the late 1990's. This has in many ways led to a lowered need to push clients to take action. That might change one day, but we are talking about re-orienting how lawyer-to-client interactions have occurred for decades. Regardless, you will get more out of your estate planning attorney if you prompt them to get together even if your only question is "is there anything we should be thinking about today or in the not-too-distant future?"

Life Insurance Agent

Life insurance products are complex, varied, and often hard to buy and maintain – at least outside of term policies. Life insurance is often seen as "I pay a premium, and you pay out to my beneficiaries when I die" arrangements. Most permanent policies are not really structured that way, though. They take tending. This misunderstanding leads to an undervaluing of what a quality life insurance advisor can bring to the table. Not every situation calls for permanent life insurance coverage, and I suppose it can be oversold – but life insurance is a tool that addresses the issue of time and liquidity in ways that other financial products and strategies typically can't. And a skilled life insurance advisor who continues to assist with the management and maintenance of coverage placed can be extremely beneficial.

Bankers

Management of cash, borrowing facilities, and even day-to-day transactions tend to get more involved the higher someone's net worth is. Consequently, a well-positioned and skilled personal banker for personal matters and commercial/business banker for business matters can smooth out a lot of hassles and boost returns and financial growth. Quality professionals on your banking team(s) can also be good connector points and issue spotters given that new opportunities often get mentioned first in the context of a banking relationship. While conversations may initially come up with other advisors too, good bankers tend to add more value to the overall situation than they are given credit for.

Business or Special Asset Advisors

This is a bit of a catchall category that is dependent on an individual, couple or family's holdings and activities. It certainly can include things like Private Equity firms and advisors, real estate agents and brokers, and the like – but also key employees within the family's business or managers of the family's real estate or other asset holdings. Involvement of these other categories can be a bit uneven during and shortly after the initial and primary wealth creation activity within a family system.

The initial wealth creator essentially fills many of these roles at the outset – and maybe for the duration. He or she is the primary business driver or the investment "picker" when it comes to real estate, operating entities, etc. The non-family advisors that one brings to the table may be more supportive of aspects of the wealth creator's activity than in a lead (at least lead advisory) role for the family. While the wealth creator may continue to be the right choice for the lead advisor position for a long stretch, a family will be well served by identifying what roles the wealth creator is filling and how they would be supplemented by other family members or third parties.

Fiduciaries

Picking an executor or trustee is something that individuals and couples tend to think of a bit one dimensionally. Who would be the right choice to handle things if something happened to them today? But the right choice changes over time and can vary based on the assets in the family's wealth system and the relative maturity, competency and interest of family members or close confidants. While a common push back to thinking beyond the immediate circumstances is "we can always change it later," you might not have the opportunity to do so down the road.

The general choices to consider for these roles are friends and family, banks and trust companies, and professional individuals like attorneys and accountants. Generally financial and investment advisors and life insurance agents are ineligible to serve in these roles, even when they would otherwise be fabulous choices, due to restrictions from their employing firms or securities regulations. Regardless, each of the categories have their pros and cons. And those pros and cons can vary over time. But no matter what, the choice will almost always have a significant impact on a family's wealth transfer activities and successes.

Family Business and/or Family System Advisors

"Family Business Advisors" and "Family System Advisors" are very broad labels. Perhaps that is because the industry norms are not completely unified and consequently so too the labels themselves – I suspect this is most so with respect to the Family Business Advisor label. Labels like these are used quite freely to mean something very different from what I'm getting at here. So what kind of advisor might fit under this category as I see it? Let me suggest a few examples:

1. There are professionals who focus on managing the dynamics that go along with having multiple gener-

ations in a family-owned enterprise. They may come from a psychology background, an academic background, or some branch of the financial services industry – and could have a particular bent to their advice depending on their previous experience before starting into this work.

2. Some advisors in this space have come out of family businesses themselves. Curiously, it seems to me that they tend not to come from the first-generation position. Even so, their personal experience in multi-generational business environments can help bridge understanding between generations within a family business.

3. Family System Advisors, as I think of them, spend more time on the governance structures within families than they would on the financial and tax implications of family transitions. And they may also be more inclined to focus on the mechanics of how a family engages in running their shared assets than in addressing specific relational dynamics between family members or the generations. The further down the road – in terms of generations – and the more connected everyone is, the more likely you and your family will see the need for this type of advisor.

4. Sometimes this person is really a type of business coach for one or more family members experiencing or participating in a generational wealth transition.

This isn't specifically a family business book – although I recognize that many business owning families will have a keen interest in the overall issues we're addressing. So, I hope that touching on the overall flavor of advisory positions specific to that circumstance is useful. But it is just a start.

Wise Friends

The most successful wealth transitions I've seen and been a part of or witness to seem to have some wise friends in the background. I've shared the difficulties associated with opening up on matters of wealth in earlier chapters, but those that do so with other similarly situated friends and colleagues seem to have better results on average. Perhaps that's because they get a nugget or two from what their friend or friends have seen. Perhaps it's the openness to seek the input of wise friends that leads to better outcomes within a family. But it's a notable enough difference in results that I do think it worth including in this list.

On the other hand, not every friend's ideas turn out to be good ideas. Or at least not good ideas for you and your family. I have had many conversations that start with something like "our friend, 'Joe' did X, Y and Z for his family, and it worked out great." And maybe it did. But that doesn't mean it will work out well for you and your family or that there aren't other, better ideas for you all either. And maybe "Joe" could have accomplished more than he thought possible given limitations on the advice and counsel that he had available to him. It goes without saying that one size definitely does not fit all when it comes to successful wealth transfers across generations.

Let's say you've selected who should be on your team. Do they need to work together? How do you make that happen?

I was recently in a meeting with a number of advisors around the table for a client facing a difficult situation. The openness to discuss and consider the various perspectives around the table, and the alignment of values, was striking and encouraging. It felt like the Holy Grail of teamwork that advisors often talk about which leads to a fully functioning estate and financial plan with skilled advisors in all the right spots contributing in their primary area of expertise, all in complete sync with the other skilled advisors in the other important disciplines. This kind of experience does not happen nearly enough.

It's often not all that practical to accomplish. Even the very wealthy, who would presumably have the greatest need for it, rarely have exceptionally high-functioning planning teams. There are other reasons for this, but a lot of it has to do with simple math. As the next illustration shows, the bigger the advisory team, the more connections need to be made to keep everyone connected. Start to count the lines of connection and it's easy to see how breakdowns is almost inevitable. The more advisors to keep connected, the easier and more likely for communication to be incomplete or inefficient.

Legal

Documents and legal structure have significant impact on family.

Business Advisors

Inside and outside advisors are important to business owning families.

Accounting

Personal, business and transfer taxes must all be accounted for.

Fiduciaries

Whether individual or corporate, fiduciaries must implement plan.

Financial

Proper investment and financial planning, the right structure, is key.

Insurance

Risk, liquidity, income replacement and other factors can be critical.

Further complicating the problem is that it is very easy for one advisor (even when well meaning) to override the good planning of another. For example, a banker or financial advisor who favors joint accounts for spouses may unwittingly side-step a thoughtful trust arrangement put together by the estate planning attorney. If you can't get everyone communicating, then you will likely need to make sure that the needed advice is coming from the right source. Legal issues should be resolved by the estate planning attorney. Investment allocation decisions in a portfolio should be sourced to the investment and financial professionals. And so on.

Getting everyone on the same page will always add value – and generally will be of greater benefit the higher the net worth. This means that the family should either take on the task of coordinating efforts or setting common meetings and conversations or appoint someone to serve that role. Some families can do this well, but generally it does seem like the meetings don't come together, don't have staying power, or are abandoned due to the frustrating nature of herding busy people to meet and communicate (sometimes complicated by geographic distance among the stakeholders). This is in part because it does take a sense of the relevant, technical planning matters to set agendas, frame issues, and motivate and organize the right people to be at any particular meeting. An outside party serving in this role can be really helpful - but they do have to be the right outside party.

Ideally, in any joint meeting, everyone at the table will have the opportunity to add value while also helping ensure that the family and its own, self-identified goals drive activity. And if you get good, skilled, kind people around the table with complementary skills and a willingness and interest in playing nice in the same sandbox with others, then almost everything can take care of itself. Let's move on then to what might need to be on your upcoming agendas.

NEXT STEPS

- Put a list together of who is on your team and also what roles are missing. If there are any gaps, fill them. If there are any needed adjustments, make them.

- Think about how connected each of your advisors is to each of your other advisors. Are any deficiencies in connectedness material? If so, how will you address any concerns you determine exist?

- Communicate your primary goals to your advisory team. Start simply if you need to, but keep those goals front and center whenever a major decision is being made or transaction suggested.

- Look for opportunities to connect your next generation members to your current advisory team. Sometimes they'll want their own advisors - which is fine and can work well. But there should be coordination among them all, and that probably is mostly likely to occur with the initiation of the older generations.

- Give serious attention to the suggested to-do's in the next chapter. They are supportive and in extension of the Follow Ups suggested here and in the previous chapters.

14

Moving Forward

L et's take stock of where we're at here at the close of our conversation. We've discussed the challenges that come with having, receiving, and transferring wealth. We've talked about how to define successful stewardship of wealth across generations. We've covered who is responsible for different parts of achieving that success. From there, we dipped our toes into contextualizing these topics with family members at various stages in their financial and personal maturity. And lastly, we discussed how best to involve advisors and other individuals to help you and your family achieve your goals.

In many ways, that's a lot. Especially if you've gotten into the nitty gritty of working with your family to define and memorialize your goals, values, and philosophies about these matters. But of course it's not enough to know the problem. It's not enough to know what success looks like. It's not enough to know the challenges. You've got to move towards success. You've got to work through the obstacles that arise. You've got to get to where you want to get. And you can't sit on your hands and expect things to work themselves out.

Working primarily in the US context, I know many people here desperately want to know "the formula." Give them a to-do list with defined steps and an order to them, and they're generally happy. I'm going to do that here – after all, if I've just described you, I want you to be happy. But before I do so, I can't emphasize enough that you'll need to fill in all kinds of sub-steps. You'll need to reverse course sometimes and re-do tasks or activities that you thought were complete but weren't or became undone. You'll need to add and subtract big things to your personal to-do list. And everyone will need to cycle back to square one at least once every successive generation. Each generation won't start with a blank slate, of course – but they'll need to reaffirm ownership of tasks, reassign responsibilities to later generations, and confirm and refine family objectives and goals, until the next generation ends up doing the same thing for whatever life looks like for them and the family at that point in time. It's a process, not a project. But it might help to start the process by having a project-looking to-do list. So let me give it a shot.

- Create a Family Wealth Statement or at least a memorialization of what virtues and values are important to you and others in your family system that are mature enough to participate in its development.

Some of you will hate this step. Or at least some members of your family will. Do it anyway. You will be glad to have gone through the exercise eventually. Trust me.

Also, because this might feel too soft and squishy for some, and some won't be as comfortable with this kind of wordsmithing, resist the temptation to just sign off on what someone else slides in front of you. Make sure that what is stated is "owned" by you as a family.

• Create a statement/document/collection of documents that summarize the family's holdings.

Even if it's not time to share this information with anyone else in the family, this summary will be an important document that will enable your advisors to give you good and complete advice. And don't do what many might be tempted to do when preparing financial statements for a bank or some other third party — understate asset values. Many of the folks I work with have made it a practice to understate values with the thought that being ultra conservative with valuations won't get them in trouble with their banks or lending providers whereas overstating or inadvertent overstating might. Putting a thumb "under the scale" may put your advisors at a bigger disadvantage than you might realize. Help them help you.

• Assemble the team.

Whether you've already identified all the players needed, or there's some work to be done, you probably haven't connected your advisors in a way where they can all synergistically provide advice and value to you and your family. As you get your team acting as a team, be conscious of who is going to coordinate the team's efforts, track progress, and have responsibility for keeping others on task and on time.

Consider who else should be at the table along the way. Consider whether you need team members that aren't as tied to you or whether the advisory team can do some or all advisory tasks for multiple family members.

- Communicate your goals to the team.

  This should ideally be accomplished with all participating family stakeholders communicating these matters to the whole advisory team. It may seem somewhat formal or ritualistic, but this is an important part of the process. You will also want to make sure that you're open to adjusting the goals as a family and to feedback from the advisory team. But you also want to avoid goal drift. In other words, you want each advisor to be able to directly and definitively state how their work is furthering which of your family's specific goals. If they can't or won't do that, they should indicate any issues they perceive with the goals in question or withdraw from the team. That sounds harsh, and would almost never happen – but putting it this firmly will help secure more alignment in the work done by the various advisors on your team.

- Set tasks and timelines.

  I said I was going to give you a project type to-do list as opposed to a process type to-do list. And I'm doing that, but this part of the effort might benefit from its own set of tasks and timelines – the development of which would be a joint effort of you, your family, and your advisory team.

  - Update legal structures to reflect newly stated goals and thinking.

  - Consider initiating wealth transfer strategies currently or set expected timelines for doing so.

  - Evaluate the manner in which investments are allocated in light of long-term family goals and the initiation in the near term of any wealth transfer strategies. This includes allocations into or out of family business and investment real estate holdings.

  - Identify structural or other threats to achieving the family's vision of success and consider strategies to mute their effect or to eliminate them altogether.

  - Establish communication timelines – at least loosely – and levels of communication for any non-participating family stakeholders. The question of levels of communication and involvement of in-laws should be addressed as part of this process. For clarity, this includes setting expected timeframes for pulling next generation members into the conversation when the time is right.

❧ Have the advisory team suggest and explore additional benefits and efficiencies that might be gained by coordinating efforts in various disciplines across generations.

❧ Establish a "check in" cadence for the full team. Do what's right for you, but if you can pull it off, I would suggest a quarterly cadence for the first year or two, not less than twice for the next year or two, and not less than annually thereafter.

❧ At the end of the meeting, ask all participants what they feel might be missing that should be addressed at the next meeting. Things will come up along the way, particularly in the earlier meetings, that you'll want to capture.

Most of these "sub-tasks" will not be resolvable within a single meeting. The first meeting is more about the initial assignments than full resolution of a matter. But it is important to get things moving and to start making progress.

Before moving on to the next item in the to-do list, let me re-focus on setting communication timelines. This is a big deal. And because you might find yourself five, ten, or fifteen years away from bringing a child or grandchild into these kinds of family discussions, it can be easy to lose track of what you should be doing along the way. Don't. Stay disciplined every step of the way, on what you should be doing today, when you should start doing something different, and when a particular individual should be fully brought into the regular flow. These preparatory steps are too important to let them slide.

- Hold a family-only check in meeting.

   This check-in meeting should consider how the prior experience with the advisory team felt and how everything discussed would be expected to meet the family's needs. I suggest that it is important to have this include family only because the ultimate responsibility for all of this is the family's. If you're a single parent wealth creator and it's too early to bring the kids fully into the conversation, grab a pen and a notepad and review how the team functioned, whether anyone had any trouble with the expressed goals, etc. Keep and refer back to your prior notes.

- Hold a team check in meeting.

   As suggested above, you should have established a cadence for gathering the family and advisory team. Perhaps the first follow up meeting will serve as that check in meeting with the advisory team – but I would suggest scheduling a separate check-in meeting to get the advisory team's feedback as well as to share what might have come from the family-only check in meeting.

- Put annual meetings on the calendar to evaluate, adjust or re-affirm the goals, review changes in financial and family circumstances, and evaluate progress status for agreed upon tasks and efforts.

In addition to the discipline of stepping back once a year, I also strongly suggest that a family should plan to do a deep dive on everything laid out above every five years. You may find it appropriate to have a special 10-year meeting cycle, too, in order to bring additional family members into the discussion more fully and seek their input more tangibly as they reach established milestones, etc.

That's not too overwhelming a list, is it? No doubt you recognize that there's a lot going on underneath the surface of most of the items above. That shouldn't be too surprising. We're trying to accomplish big things. Big things that are not easy to accomplish. But I hope you find the outline of what to do pretty simple.

Would it help if I tried to make it simpler? If so, how does this strike you:

Agree. Align. Act.

Adjust and Re-Align. Act.

Adjust and Re-Align. Act.

And so on.

OK. Fair enough. I didn't make it easier. I just made it shorter. But if it helps you get started, let's just say I made it simpler. After all, if you get started and have a bit of persistence, I am confident you can accomplish great things in your family!

15

Final Thoughts

I am really happy that you picked up this book and read it through. In doing so, you allowed me to have a conversation with you about an important, personal subject. That probably means you're someone who cares about the long-term health and well-being of those you love and care for. Conversations like these with people like you have been one of the most rewarding things for me, both personally and professionally. Thank you!

This book was birthed from a realization that too many people with wealth were scared about what an inheritance might do to their children and grandchildren, too many were unsettled as to whether their plan was the right one, and too many were confused as to where things stand or even where to begin at all. Speaking to this realization in living rooms, conference rooms, hotel ballrooms and elsewhere made it clear that we're really worried about ruining our kids (and grandkids, etc.) with money. And we know that we only get one shot at doing our part in this multi-generational project – so there is significant pressure on us.

But here we are. Talking about it. And I hope I've given you some handholds and ideas and encouragement to take action along with some language and perspective to engage with your family and your advisory team. And with that, I hope you're now able to take whatever motivation that led you to read this book through to start making tangible progress toward doing more good with the wealth that your family is responsible for managing today and in the future. I'm excited to see what you all will accomplish together!

Glossary

While most of the words included in this short glossary might be known to you, there may be some nuances in the context of our primary subject that make their definitions worth fleshing out a bit more. Where the definitions are more obvious, I'll focus on the nuances.

Advisors – Obviously you know what advisors are – although you should understand what experience, training, and expertise each person giving you advice is. While each advisor should know what their primary focus should be, you may also benefit from their broader perspective and experience, too. Watch for additional resources to help get the most out of your advisors, too, at www.markshiller.com/resources.

Advisory Team – An advisory team is your collection of advisors for your personal family and financial situation. They may never have gathered, but each professional or confidant you look to with respect to these matters is part of a team whether they know it or not. Best if they do know each other, though!

Business Succession Plan – A Business Succession Plan is a plan to deal with the succession of ownership, management, and benefits associated with a closely-held business. Although these different levels of succession are not always considered separately, they all have different implications. Who takes over as President of the family's company might be different from who receives the shares in the company by gift or at the death of the present owners. Some of these plans might be informally discussed, while other aspects might be formally memorialized in a buy-sell agreement or other similar documentation.

Dynasty Trust – I've never really liked the term "Dynasty Trust" as it feels like it plays to a narcissistic mentality. I prefer "continuing trusts" or something along those lines. Regardless, the term is out there and used by many. In short, it means a trust that is designed to last for either a really, really long time and potentially forever. We're talking generations and hundreds or even thousands of years. Whether they do or not is another matter – but the idea is that the continuation of the trust structure will be protective of family assets and allow future heirs to enjoy and benefit from those assets far into the future.

Estate Plan – There are many definitions to what an estate plan is. For an estate planning attorney, and therefore the way I usually think of it, an estate plan is a collection of legal documents and structures that addresses the management of an individual, couple or family's personal, health, and financial decisions. Generally, the documents in question will be applicable while the document creators are fully competent and capable – but will also address the implications of death or disability and how wealth passes to identified heirs and beneficiaries thereafter.

Estate Tax – An estate tax is a tax on the transfer of property from a deceased person to that person's beneficiaries. Many "developed" countries have such a tax, including the United States, but certainly not all. Usually there is an exemption from that tax, which means that estates that are worth less than that exemption do not have to pay any estate tax. In the United States, that exemption is $13,610,000 in 2024, but scheduled to drop to about half of that in 2026.

Family Wealth Statement – There are other terms for this – you might hear "Family Constitution" or "Family Compact" as a couple of examples. In short, though, it is a memorialization of what is important and central to a particular family's view of wealth. Although some are "imposed" on the family, the best Family Wealth Statements are documents that evolve and remain core to future generations' view of stewarding family wealth and incorporate input from multiple generations.

Fiduciary – A fiduciary is someone who has responsibilities over something or someone for another person's benefit. For instance, a trustee, who controls the management of assets for the beneficiary or beneficiaries of a trust, is a fiduciary as to those beneficiaries. The law imposes duties and obligations on the fiduciary in recognition of the fact that they have a position of power and need to be accountable for any abuses of that power.

Financial Advisor – Financial advisors come in many shapes, sizes, and varieties. Generally speaking, though, a financial advisor is a professional who is paid to offer financial advice to clients. While their focus might be on things as varied as budgeting and sophisticated investment strategies, financial advisors assist with the management and utilization of your assets. Many will be licensed and regulated professionals, and many will also carry certifications and designations applicable to their areas of expertise.

Financial Plan – A financial plan is usually focused on a single individual or couple's personal spending and investment planning. It often accounts for tax implications, major spending needs, risk management, retirement planning, and ultimately the disposition of the individual or couple's holdings to their desired beneficiaries.

Gen 1, Gen 2, Gen 3 . . . – References like these in the book – and in a fair amount of literature regarding family wealth – simply are short-hands for referring to members of a particular generation relative to another or to the total membership in a generation. So if we're referring to someone who is a Gen 2, their parent will be a Gen 1 and their children will be a Gen 3. Note that some will abbreviate things even further – G1, G2, and G3 and so on.

Generation-Skipping Transfer Tax – The generation-skipping transfer tax, or GST tax, is an additional transfer tax in the United States that applies to transfers to individuals more than one generation younger than the transferor. A gift from a grandparent to a grandchild "skips" the child's generation and would be subject to the GST tax. This tax was instituted as a way to "protect" estate taxation, or more directly, estate tax revenue. There is an exemption from the GST tax, but otherwise the net effect is to cause a tax roughly equivalent to what the estate tax would be at each generation.

Gift Tax – Gift tax is applied to gifts made from one person to another, whether directly or indirectly, during lifetime. There is usually an exemption from this tax, and sometimes the exemption is tied to who the donee/recipient is in relationship to the donor/giver. For instance, gifts to a spouse may not incur a gift tax whereas a gift to a child would. In the United States, the exemption from the estate tax and gift tax are connected – meaning the use of a $1 of gift taxes will reduce the estate tax exemption by $1.

Goals – You don't need a definition for "goals." In this book, though, when considering goals we're usually thinking of bigger, broader, and multi-generational family goals and not more discrete goals like buying a vacation home or retiring with a certain asset level or income stream. So goals in this book would generally be thought of as lifetime and beyond goals. What goals would you want to have accomplished if you were at the end of your life looking back? Those are the kind of goals we're dealing with here.

Investment Advisor – Investment Advisors and Financial Advisors are sometimes terms used interchangeably. See Financial Advisors above for that common definition. Where Investment Advisors are distinct from Financial Advisors, though, would be when they truly focus solely on the selection of investments in a portfolio and not on the planning associated with the portfolio or total assets of an individual, couple or family.

Legal Structures – In this book, legal structures are anything that establish a framework for the ownership, management and benefit associated with an individual, couple's or family's assets. This can include things like Wills and Trusts, corporations, limited liability companies, shareholder agreements, family compacts, and so on.

Liquidity Event – A sale or other transaction that leads to a dramatic increase in cash or otherwise easy to spend assets, such as the sale of a privately-held business or real estate property or portfolio. Although originally in the book, I removed the term "Liquidity Event" from the text because it isn't a term everyone has heard before. However, in families of wealth, Liquidity Events are potentially life altering, so I include the definition here.

Next Gens – Next Gens generally would be thought of as members of generations younger than the present holders of family wealth.

Power of Attorney – an estate planning technique where someone (the "principal") appoints another (usually referred to as the "agent") to make specific financial or health care related decisions for him or herself.

Rising Generation – I didn't refer to this in the text of this book, but you'll likely see this term (or the shorter Rising Gen's) as a short-hand for the generations who are not too far off from being contributing stakeholders within a family's system.

Senior Generation – The Senior Generation is comprised of members of a generation that either holds the primary stewardship of family wealth or once did. More generally, it could also refer to the older or oldest generation as to a particular question, topic or discussion.

Trust – A trust is a legal structure formed by an individual (referred to often as the Settlor or Grantor or Donor) by transferring assets to a trustee who will have a fiduciary duty to manage the assets for the benefit of beneficiaries chosen by the Settlor. Trusts can be revocable (i.e., changeable by the Settlor) or irrevocable (i.e., unchangeable by the Settlor). There is a great variety of trust structures, but they all have this general construction. Note that the US context utilizes trusts much more frequently than in almost any other national jurisdiction.

Trustee – A trustee is a fiduciary who is responsible for managing the assets of a trust for the benefit of the trust's beneficiaries.

Values – Values are attributes, traits and qualities that someone views as good and desirable. In contrast to virtues, values tend to be more subjective and not universal. However, there may be some values that rise to the level of virtues within a family or culture even if not viewed as universally good and desirable. *See,* www.markshiller.com/resources for more resources on values and how to identify your and your family's values.

Virtues – Virtues are attributes, traits and qualities that all would view as universally, or nearly universally, good and desirable. Unlike values, virtues are objectively considered positive – although the importance placed on each might vary individual to individual, family to family, or culture to culture. *See,* www.markshiller.com/resources for more resources on virtues and how to identify what are primary virtues for you and your family.

Wealth Transfer Strategies – Wealth Transfer Strategies is a broad term that encompasses legal and financial strategies and structures to effectively and efficiently transfer stewardship and benefit of personal and family wealth usually from one generation to another. Some of these strategies can get quite complex, while others might be as simple as writing a check or handing over shares in a family corporation to your child.

Will – A Will is a legal document that provides for the disposition of assets held by an individual at that individual's death. It may or may not be the primary document to accomplish this disposition, but is sometimes thought of as a colloquial conflation of a person's general wishes for how their assets will be divided and distributed at death.

Additional Resources

At several points along the way, you will have seen a reference to additional resources. Although it is my hope that How to Not Ruin Your Kids with Money is of great help in and of itself, there are so many more things to consider and work through – more than could be included in a single, written work. So please visit www.markshiller.com/resources or use the QR Code below to learn about additional resources that may be of help to you and your family on your journey. There will be a spot for you to recommend additional resources that could be of help to others, too.

Use this QR Code to access the additional resources at
www.markshiller.com/resources

Public Speaking

How to Not Ruin Your Kids with Money is in part a response to the enthusiasm of audiences for Mark's presentations on the topic. Great audiences for this keynote and related presentations include:

Investment Firms/Professionals and their clients and prospects

Law Firms and Accounting Firms and their clients and prospects

Banks, Investment Banks, and Insurance Firms and their clients and prospects

Family Business Organizations and Centers

Multi-Family Offices and Similar Organizations

Charitable Organizations and Associations

Professional Associations, like Estate Planning Councils

Conferences

Industry/Trade Associations

To learn more and determine availability, please contact Aevitas Press at speakers@aevitaspress.com or use the QR Code below to learn more about presentation options and to initiate a conversation about bringing Mark in to speak at your next event.

Reviews and Feedback

Thank you for reading *How to Not Ruin Your Kids with Money*. I hope I've shared something of personal value and impact with you in these pages. I'm also guessing that you might have some things to say that could make any updated version of this book or future books more beneficial and useful. If so, I would love to hear from you at mark@markshiller.com!

In addition, honest, positive reviews on Amazon and elsewhere not only help me know what is of value to you, but also help others find this book and get further on their journey. I would be honored if you would take a couple of minutes to leave a review and a bit about what you thought of this book by visiting markshiller.com/review or using the QR code below.

Thank you!

Use this QR Code to initiate your review of
How to Not Ruin Your Kids with Money

Use of This Book

Although the author and publisher have made every effort to ensure that the information in this book was correct at press time, the author and publisher do not assume and hereby disclaim any liability to any party for any loss, damage, or disruption caused by errors or omissions, whether such errors or omissions result from negligence, accident, or any other cause.

Adherence to all applicable laws and regulations, including international, federal, state and local governing professional licensing, business practices, advertising, and all other aspects of doing business in the US, Canada or any other jurisdiction is the sole responsibility of the reader and consumer.

Neither the author nor the publisher assumes any responsibility or liability whatsoever on behalf of the consumer or reader of this material.

Any perceived slight of any individual or organization is purely unintentional.

The resources in this book are provided for informational purposes only and should not be used to replace the specialized training and professional judgment of appropriate financial, tax, legal, mental health care or other appropriate professionals. Neither the author nor the publisher may be held responsible for the use of the information provided within this book. Readers should use their own judgment and consult appropriate professionals before making and finalizing any decision regarding planning for their individual circumstances.

Order Additional Copies

To assist you and others in having fuller and more productive conversations within your families regarding stewarding wealth across generations, you can visit www.markshiller.com/sales/ or use the QR Code below to purchase more copies and related materials.
If you have any questions regarding purchasing directly from the author or Aevitas Press, you are welcome to email info@aevitaspress.com.

Use this QR Code to order additional copies of
How to Not Ruin Your Kids with Money
for your friends, family, and advisors

Made in the USA
Monee, IL
05 November 2024

60cd2843-85d8-41c2-973c-74461126efd2R01